DOLLMAKING
ONE ARTIST'S APPROACH

DOLLMAKING
ONE ARTIST'S APPROACH
BY
ROBERT McKINLEY

Editor
Linda Nelson

Designer
Les Derby

Production Coordinator
Bill Nelson

Publisher
McKinley Books

*This book is dedicated to Gene Moore
and to my beloved Miriam Golombeck,
the two people who were the first to call
me an artist and my work, art.*

Acknowledgments

I always thought that to write a book one just sat down and wrote it. That is not true. Writing a book involves a number of people and a great deal of support. I've been incredibly lucky in my life to have met a lot of wonderful people without whose help and support there would not only not be a book, but there would be no dolls. So to the following people, thank you.

Bill Nelson. I have been a fan of Bill's art for years, long before I knew him. Watching what is happening in his growth as a fine doll artist is the thrill of a lifetime.

Linda Nelson. Linda should be canonized. She actually learned to read what passes for my handwriting and pulled this manuscript together. Bless you.

Nancy and David Walters. Without these two people there would be no point in going on. If I can't talk to them at least twice a week, I go into withdrawal. Talk about a support group. WOW!

Les Derby. Succinctly put, Les is a book designing genius, and I'd trust him with my life.

Miriam Golombeck. Miriam was the first to think my work was actually worth owning.

Gene Moore. A divine man, Gene really put my work on the map through his beautiful windows at Tiffany & Co.

E.J. Taylor. I've never met E. J. Taylor, but his work was the first to show me that dolls are indeed an art form and a fine art form at that.

Van Craig. Van's work is a constant delight and constant source of inspiration to improve the way I see things with insight and humor.

Susie Oroyan. I don't think she wants it generally known, but Susi is a kind, generous, and gifted lady. Here's to you, Mama Doc.

Mike Pocklington. His beautiful color photograph perfectly captured the mood of the piece.

Bill Bodenschatz. For all the years gone by.

Bert Newman. For all the years yet to come.

Contents

Foreword

I first met Bob McKinley in New York City in the late summer of 1989. Having seen his dolls in *Dolls Magazine*, I was a little nervous about the meeting. What I didn't learn until much later was that Bob was familiar with my work as an illustrator and was nervous about the meeting, as well. We both had assumed that the other was unapproachable. Now that I have gotten to know him, I realize that the word "unapproachable" could never apply to Bob McKinley.

At the time of that first meeting with Bob I was exhibiting a group of 42" tall dolls at a gallery in Soho, and I was convinced that those dolls were the best thing I would and could ever do as a dollmaker. But within a month I abandoned those dolls forever, and with Bob's patient instruction I embarked on a whole new direction in my dollmaking. With numerous letters and diagrams and so many Polaroids that I lost count, Bob took me through each and every step of dollmaking the McKinley way. I remember how great it felt the first time I sculpted a decent hand using his techniques. My first pair of leather shoes was cause for celebration, and the first doll to find its balance and stand alone was truly thrilling to me.

But I am not the first person to whom Bob has given such detailed instruction. He has done this for others and with each person he has taken the time to outline every-thing in great detail. He doesn't believe in secrets. He has always been available to answer all questions. Now with this book he has done for each of you what he has done for me and others before me. It has taken many years for Bob to develop these techniques. Most of them he has had to devise himself because there were no books around to guide him. His willingness to share all he knows is rare. Most of us hide our methods away, afraid that someone will use our techniques and make a doll that will outshine our own. That doesn't concern Bob McKinley in the least. His comment to me when I was wrestling with this same issue was that "sharing and helping others to reach their potentials just gives us more to see".

I encourage you to put Bob's knowledge of dollmaking, presented in detail in this book, into practice. You will be surprised at what you can accomplish. You most likely will even come up with some ideas of your own. With the pages to follow you will find clear, concise diagrams and instructions and wonderful photographs that will carry you through every step of dollmaking from sculpting a head to creating a pair of leather shoes. The photographs, taken by Bob as he created a doll step by painstaking step, are even better than the Polaroids he sent me, so it stands to reason that your dolls will be better, too.

Bill Nelson

Introduction

Dollmaking, for me, is a complete art form. From concept to completion a doll requires me to be a designer, a sculptor, a painter, a dressmaker, and a hairdresser. Making a doll uses every bit of knowledge and whatever talent I possess. It can be frustrating to the extreme, but when the finishing touches go on and this creation of mine stands before me, the feelings of accomplishment and pride are indescribable and far outweigh the frustrations.

This book is an accurate account of the making of a doll. The methods used are ones I have learned and developed over the years and are the same for every doll I now make regardless of the style or the medium, except for porcelain which is a whole different ball game. The doll in this book was made with Super Sculpey, which to keep things simple, I just call Sculpey.

Every doll I make I hope will be perfect. This does not happen. Dollmaking is not an exact science, and mistakes happen. All the mistakes I made in constructing the doll in this book were photographed along with whatever had to be done to correct them. More often than not, what you aim for is not the final result. It is a constant amazement to me that something I am creating and supposedly have control over develops a life of its own and literally dictates what it will be. I sometimes think the doll knows better than I what it should be.

The photographs that follow are step-by-step and in the order in which each part of the doll was actually made. I begin with the head which is usually the most exciting part of the process. Usually a head can be roughly sculpted in about forty-five minutes, but it can take days to refine. While I am sculpting or even thinking about it, I stare at people to the point of rudeness. It is a great learning experience and one that I love.

Because of my background in the garment industry, I find developing the pattern for the body fascinating. It looks complicated, but it is not, and it always gives an accurate pattern for a cloth body with the correct form for whatever body type the doll requires. There is a good bit of hand sewing involved, but nothing fancy as far as stitches are concerned, and I never hesitate to glue when I can. The armature for the legs and feet came about because I could never get two feet to match. With the method of construction I use you may not get beautiful legs and feet, but you'll get a pair that match. It took a very long time to learn to make hands. The coil method works like a charm. It is fast and easy, and the resulting hands can be posed in any position. They can be as stylized or as realistic as you wish.

I would like to pass on one bit of wisdom taught to me by Helen Bullard, my mentor and the founding president of NIADA (National Institute of American Doll Artists). When I began to make dolls, I would do the most beautiful drawings of the finished piece in the pose I wanted with the expression I wanted, complete to the last detail. The finished doll was always a failure and I very nearly gave it all up. Helen set me on the right path. "You idiot," she said, and that is a direct quote, "never, never, sketch the finished doll. The actual doll will not be exactly like the drawing, and you will always be disappointed." She was right. I will sometimes do a rough thumbnail sketch, but no more than that. Without a master sketch governing what I do, I am free to make changes at any given point. Instead, I begin each and every doll with a diagram, actual size, of the body type and general posture. It is a drawing of a static nude figure front and side view and is used only as a reference for correct proportions and measurements.

There are, of course, as many different ways of making dolls as there are dollmakers. The methods in this book are those which work best for me. If you are an experienced dollmaker, perhaps you may glean an idea or two as I do each time I see another artist's work. If you are a novice, I envy you the adventure upon which you are about to embark. Please don't feel these instructions are to be slavishly followed. If they are, the result will be a pale copy of this doll and not your own expression of what a doll should be. Make use of what is of value and disregard what is not. Very quickly you will develop a way of doing things that is yours alone, and that is what dollmaking is all about.

Bob McKinley
New York
January, 1991

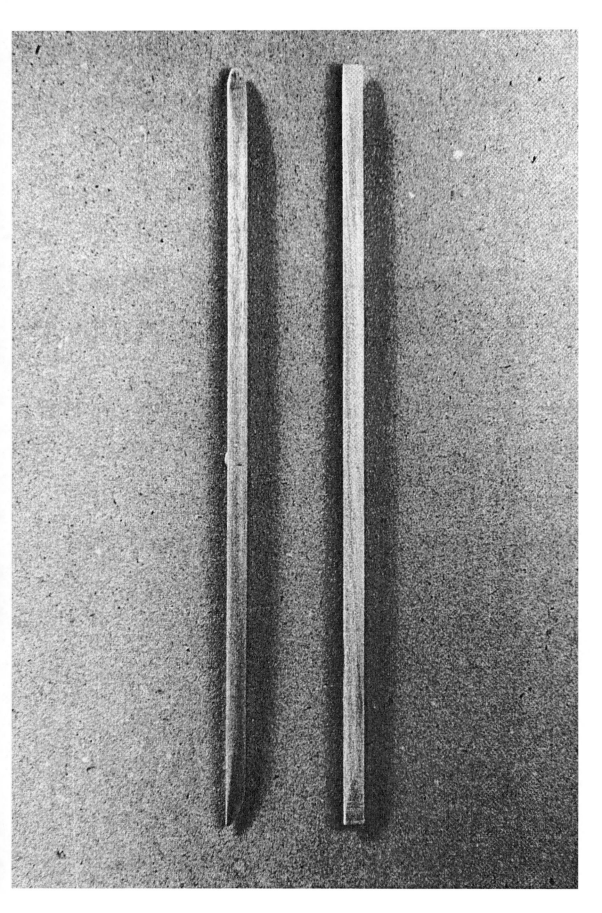

The Tool

1

The clay portions of the doll in this book were sculpted entirely with a tool made from a manicurists' orange stick. The tool was made by rounding off one end of the stick into a slightly pointed oval with sandpaper and by sanding the other end into a sharp knifelike edge. There is no point in spending vast amounts of money on expensive modeling tools when an orange stick does the trick. The orange stick has the advantage of being the perfect size for most dolls, as well as a shape which is ideal, once customized, for getting into all the nooks and crannies necessary for putting in the detail dear to the hearts of most doll artists. Once the orange stick is shaped, it is a good idea to sand it smooth with very fine sandpaper and to give it a couple of coats of paste wax for added strength. If at any time the points blunt or break off, simply reshape and re-wax.

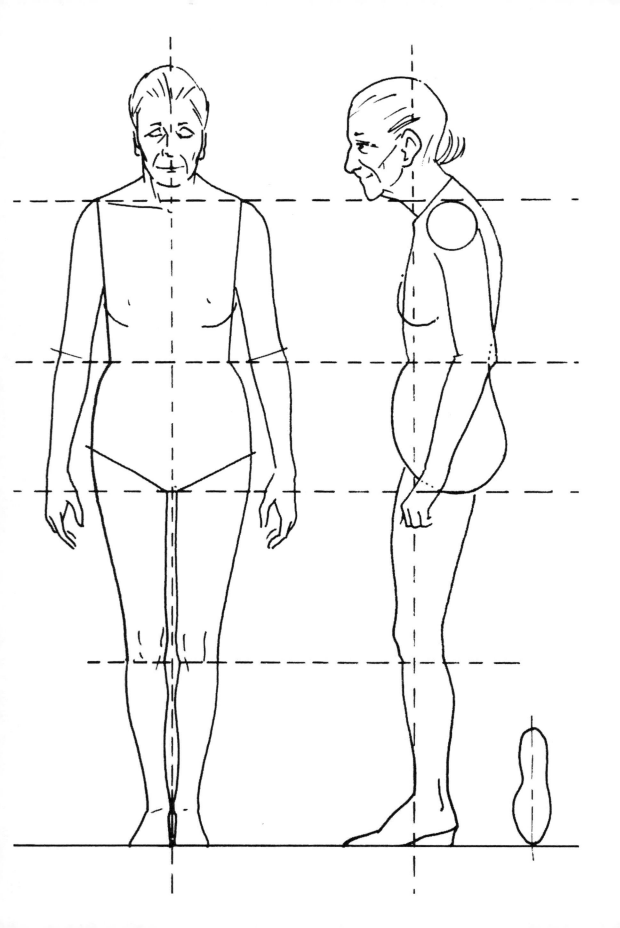

The Diagram

2

All of my dolls begin with a diagram. To do a drawing of the character or even the pose can more or less lock you into what the finished doll should look like and doesn't allow serendipitous accidents to happen which often improve the figure. The diagram I use is nothing more than a chart of proportions drawn actual size. I keep this diagram in front of me throughout the dollmaking process. It is easier for me to measure certain things with this drawing near at hand.

When developing your diagram, it is important to keep in mind certain guidelines for the correct proportions of the human figure. These guidelines may be used depending on how each individual artist "sees" the human body or imagines a particular planned doll.

The head is used universally as the unit of measurement for the body's relative proportions. For the average, ideal adult female figure, a height of 7 1/2 to eight "heads" is generally accepted. The center of the figure is about four heads from the top of the figure and falls a bit above the crotch with the remainder of the figure comprising 3 1/2 to four heads of the figure's height. A taller figure would have legs that measure four heads. A shorter figure would be shorter waisted with shorter legs. Changing the proportions slightly is part of what gives each doll its individual character. Necks can be long or short depending on what you are trying to achieve. Elbows should hit at the waist or a little above, and the wrist should fall about even with the widest part of the hips. The forearm from wrist to elbow is equal to about one head in length. From elbow to the top of the shoulder is generally 1 1/3 heads. The arm from the top of the shoulder to the finger tips reaches halfway between the crotch and the knee.

In addition to the slight variations in proportions that exist between different individual persons are the variations in a single individual's proportions at different stages in his or her life. Many changes occur in the human form as age takes its toll. The human figure may shrink up to a full head, with a woman of seventy generally measuring anywhere from 6 1/2 to seven heads in height. The spine collapses somewhat with age, the hips thrust forward slightly, the neck sinks into the chest. If you are doing an aged figure, all of this must be taken into consideration. The diagram of the doll made for the purpose of this work was altered from the average or ideal young female to a woman of about seventy. The legs are bent slightly, the waist is shortened, as are the legs, and the back is bent forward to form what is known as the dowager hump.

The diagram once established is used as a guide for all the patterns of the cloth body as well as a guide for the sculpted pieces. Slight variations do occur in constructions, but for the most part the completed doll remains true to this beginning diagram.

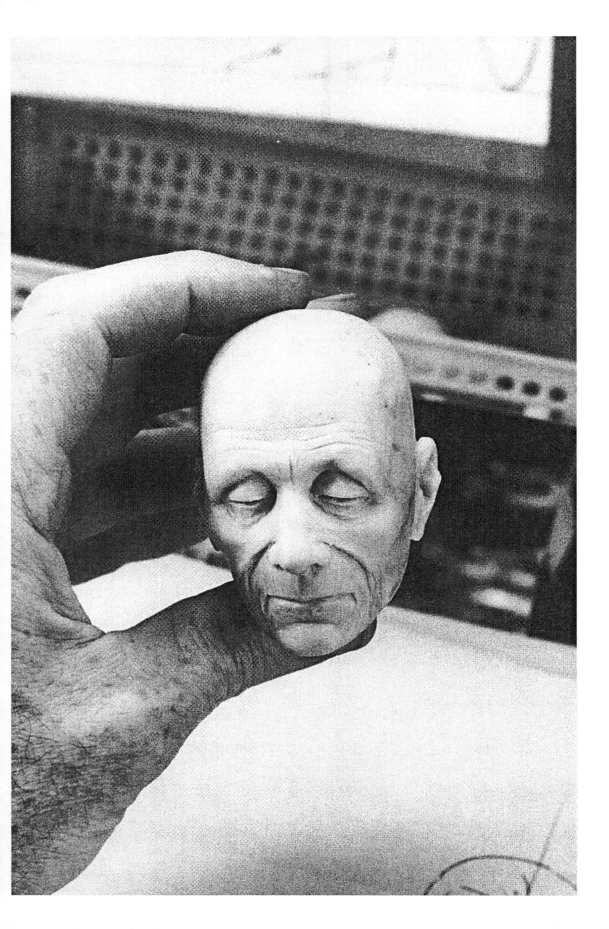

Sculpting
the Head

3

A doll is the sum total of its parts. If one part must be singled out as the most important, however, it would be the head. The head is used as the unit of measurement for the rest of the doll and its size governs the size of the finished doll.

There are a few simple rules of proportion that must be understood before you begin sculpting the head. Basically the head is shaped like an egg. The widest part of this egg shape forms the forehead, the narrowest part, the chin. On the adult face the eyes are placed halfway between the top of the head and the chin. The bottom of the nose is placed halfway between the eyes and the chin. The mouth is placed halfway between the nose and the chin. Of course, these proportions may vary slightly according to the character being sculpted. The nose may be slightly shorter, the upper lip a bit longer. Eyes placed a bit low give a young, "cute" look, etc. These variances are perfectly permissible for achieving the individual character of your doll, but they should never be so extreme as to jar the viewer or appear to be a mistake.

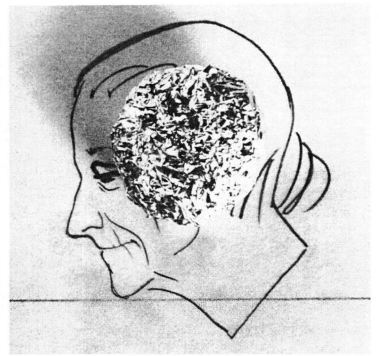

figure 1: To begin the doll's head roll aluminum foil into a ball about 1 1/4" in diameter and flatten the sides. A tracing of the head from the diagram will help you get the correct size. The flattened ball of foil does not have to be an elaborately shaped skull. It simply acts as an armature around which the head is built. It also will lessen the weight of the head and ensure that it will cure all the way through.

figure 2: Shape four 1/2" thick pieces of Sculpey large enough to cover the foil armature in four sections. A layer of paper towels on your work surface will help keep the Sculpey clean.

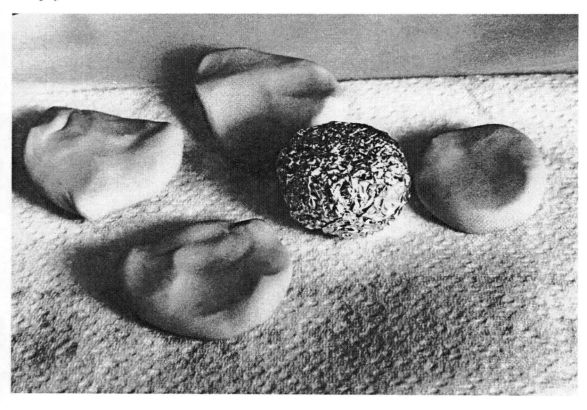

figure 3: Cover the foil armature with the pieces of Sculpey, pressing firmly.

figure 4: Smooth and blend the pieces together. Try to maintain a uniform thickness of Sculpey over the armature.

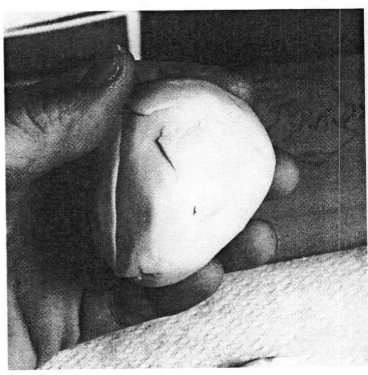

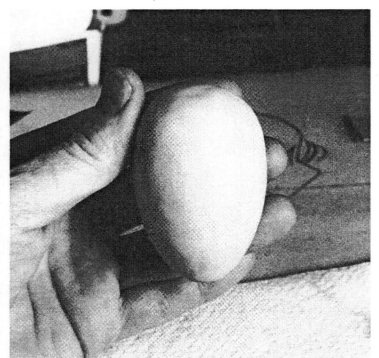

figure 5: When the pieces are blended and smoothed, begin to shape the basic egg shape of the head. Take your time doing this and try to get the egg as symmetrical as you can. If the egg shape is not symmetrical at this point, it will make placing the features of the face very difficult, if not impossible.

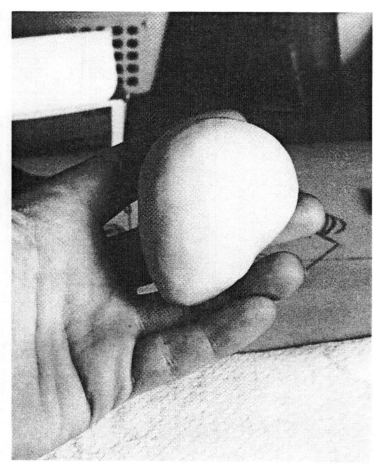

figure 6: Use your thumb to press in the back of the head and form the beginning of the jaw line.

figure 7: With the knife side of the tool draw a vertical line from the top of the head to the chin dividing the head exactly in half. Draw a line perpendicular to the vertical line dividing the head exactly in half horizontally. This horizontal line is the eye placement line. Divide the vertical line in half again from the eye line to the chin. This is the nose placement line. Then divide the vertical line in half between the nose placement line and the chin and you have the mouth line. These lines need not be deep. They should, however, be as perpendicular as possible.

figure 8: Using the knife side of the tool again, draw in the eye sockets. The sockets are roughly oval in shape and for this doll about 1/2" across, 3/8" in height and 1/4" apart. The centers of the ovals should be slightly below the eye placement line. These measurements are approximate, but both ovals or sockets for a particular doll should be the same size. A small calipers helps ensure symmetry, but the eyes' relative size can usually be determined visually.

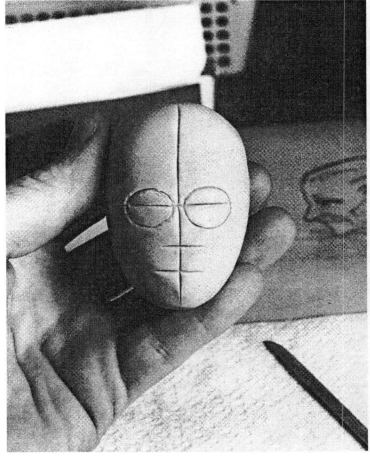

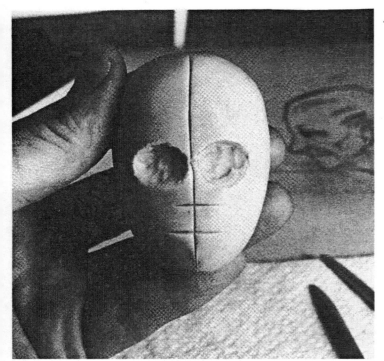

figure 9: Using the oval end of the tool, hollow out the eye sockets about 3/8" deep at the inner corners, a bit less at the outer corners.

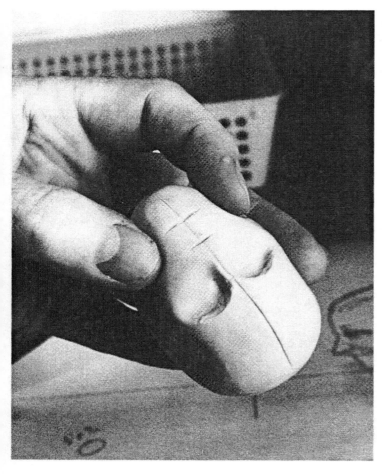

figure 10: Smooth the lower edges of the eye sockets into the cheek area leaving the brow ridge sharp. With your thumb and forefinger squeeze the area just beneath the cheekbones, creating hollows.

figure 11: Repeat the same squeezing procedure to form the temples. The head at this point is beginning to resemble a skull. You can deepen the hollows if you wish or make them more subtle.

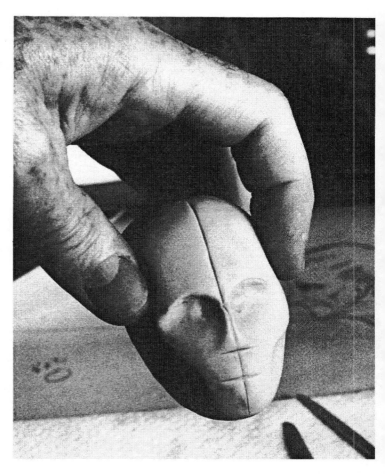

figure 12: Roll a ball of Sculpey about the size of a pea, larger or smaller depending on the size you want the nose to be. I tend toward large, high-ridged noses because I find them more interesting to sculpt.

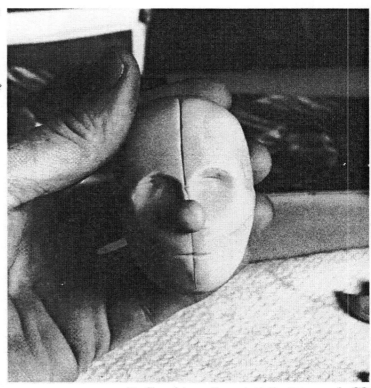

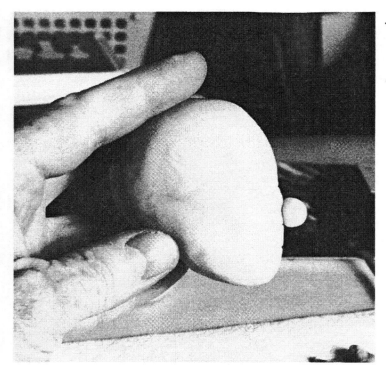

figure 13: Place the ball of Sculpey dead center on the vertical dividing line and just above the horizontal nose placement line.

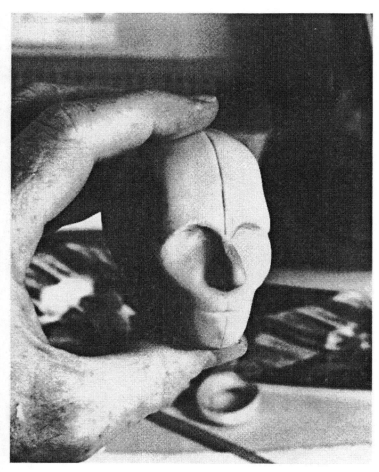

figure 14: Smooth the ball of clay up from the tip of the nose to the brow ridge and from the tip toward the sides of the head.

figure 15: The bridge and nostrils begin to form.

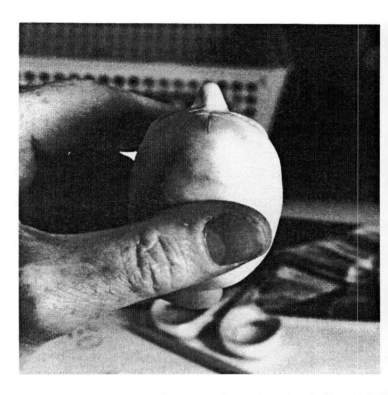

figure 16: Push the knife end of the tool into each side of the nose about 1/4", pushing the knife to the side to form each nostrll.

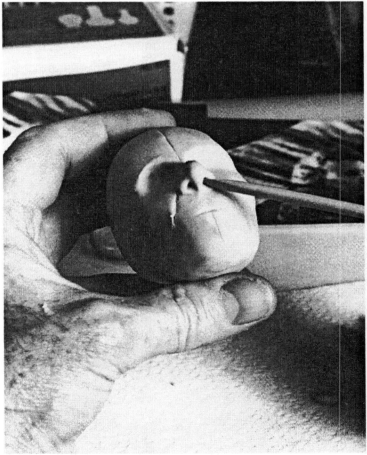

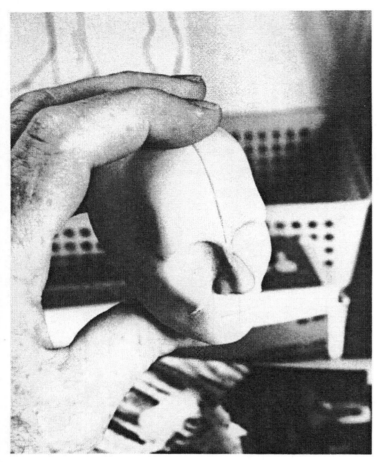

figure 17: Pushing the tool into the nose will not only form the nostrils, but the bulb end of the nose, as well . At this point it is all very rough, but keep symmetry in mind. Make both nostrils the same depth and the same shape.

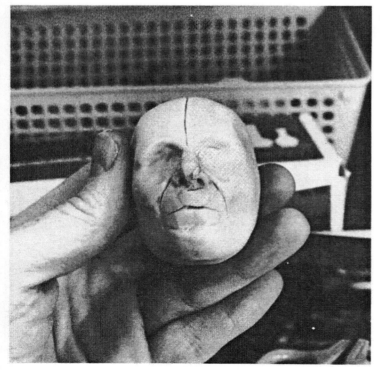

figure 18: Add little pats of Sculpey to the nose to even out the shape.

figure 19: Once the nostrils are formed, draw the age lines that form from the sides of the nose down to just beyond the corners of the mouth and press in to round out the mouth area. The corners of the mouth are deeper than the center. A little pat placed in the center of the upper lip area above the mouth line and one placed below the mouth line help keep the center of the mouth round.

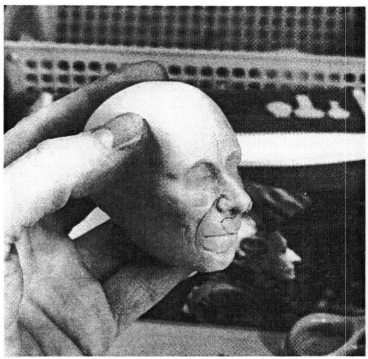

figure 20: Refine the now roughed in nose and mouth. Little pats of Sculpey are placed where they are needed. Here pats were placed on the sides of the nose to form the buttress that exists at the bridge. The flesh on either side of the nostrils running down to the corners of the mouth has been exaggerated a bit. The lips are formed by placing the knife edge of the tool on the mouth line and pushing down to form the lower lip. This old gal has rather thin lips, not much more than the line drawn for the mouth placement. Indicate the little indentation at the center of the upper lip and deepen the corners.

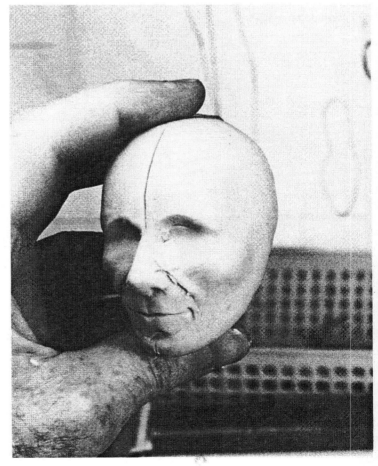

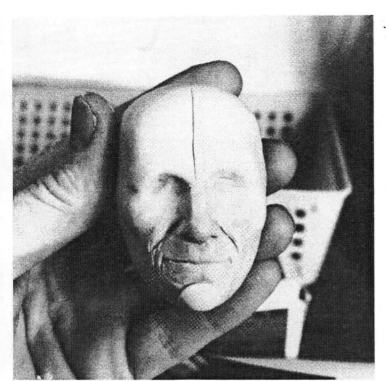

figure 21: Roll out a ball of Sculpey a bit larger than a pea.

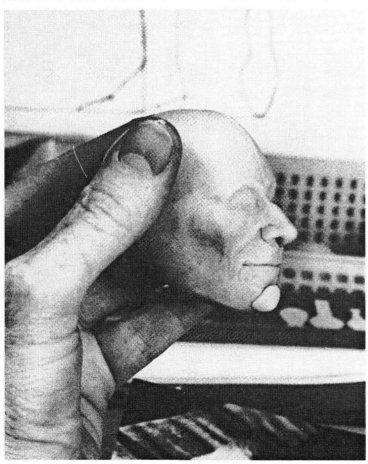

figure 22: Flatten it slightly and put it on the chin.

figure 23: Smooth the chin in place. Deepen the line that is about halfway between the mouth and the chin.

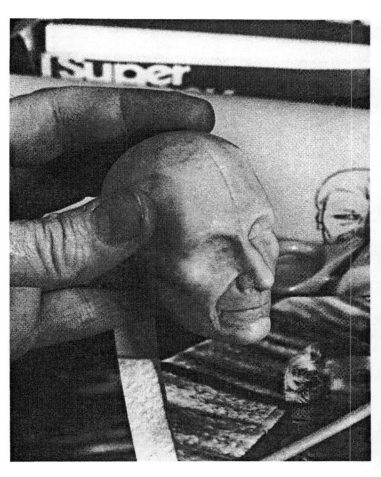

figure 24: Re-draw the eye placement lines which were lost in smoothing the eye sockets. Be very careful to keep them on the same level. This for some reason is difficult to do. Check by looking at the head turned upside down or by holding it up to a mirror. Correct the lines at this point if necessary.

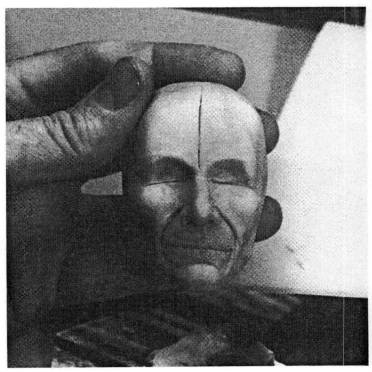

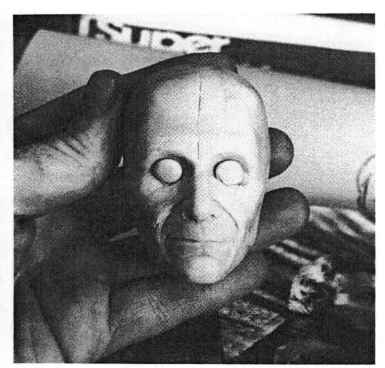

figure 25: Roll out two balls of Sculpey, again about the size of two peas and as close to the same size as possible. Flatten them just a bit and place them in the sockets. Press in firmly.

figure 26: Smooth the balls into the sockets around the edges keeping them round. Draw a line where the upper and lower lids meet. This head will be looking down so the eye will appear to be closed. Another general rule of proportion—the space between the eyes is equal to the width of one eye.

figure 27: Roll out two oval pats of Sculpey about 1/4" long. Getting the right size here is basically a trial and error process. Place the ovals just below the brow ridge, touching the upper, outer corner of each eyeball. These form the drooping areas that happen with age.

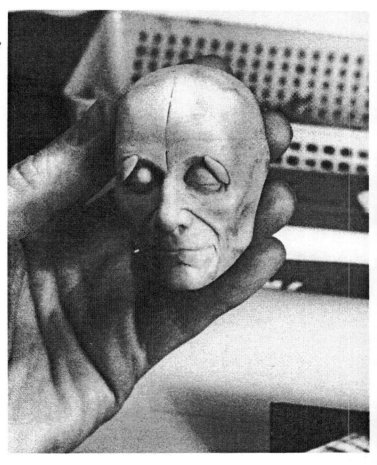

figure 28: Smooth the ovals into the surrounding areas. Put the knife edge of the tool into the lid line and open the eye slightly by pushing down. Form the bags beneath the eyes by pressing in the area beneath each of them. Begin to draw in the wrinkles at the corners of the eyes with the knife edge. When you do something to one eye, immediately do the same thing to the other.

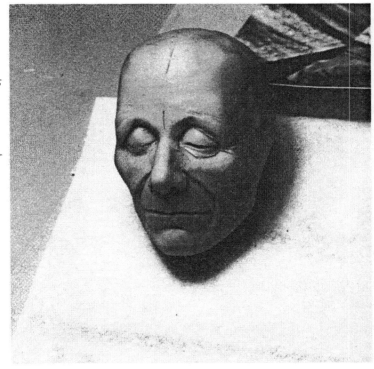

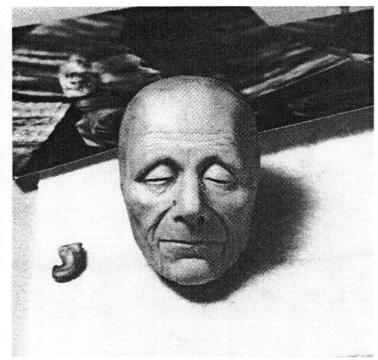

figure 29: When the eyes and wrinkles are the way you want them, begin to smooth the surface. A camel hair or sable watercolor brush dipped in fingernail polish remover and brushed gently across the head will smooth away blemishes. Acetone and lacquer thinner can also be used but are dangerous to your health. Use precautions when using them. Avoid breathing the fumes and any prolonged contact with your skin. Be careful with whatever solvent you use that you don't brush away your details.

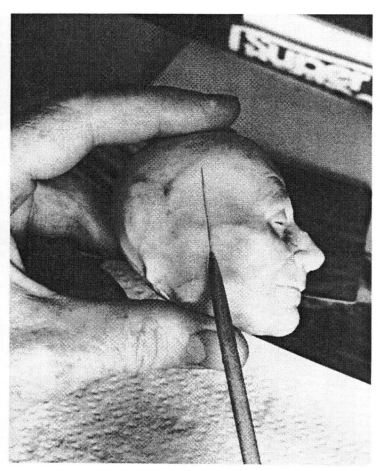

figure 30: To place the ears imagine a straight line from forehead to chin. The ear placement line is roughly halfway between the front of the face and the back of the head and is parallel to the front of the head. Draw the vertical ear line parallel to that.

figure 31: The back of the head begins to curve at the ear line. With your thumb pull the clay down to form the beginning of the neck and jaw line.

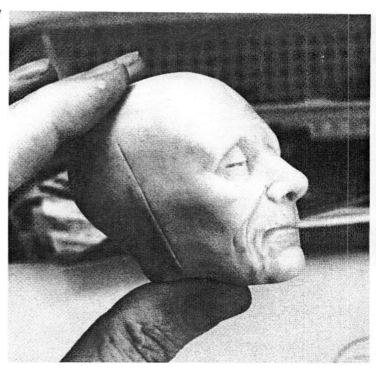

figure 32: Mark a line perpendicular to the vertical ear line a little above the corner of the eye. Mark another at approximately the bottom of the nose. The earhole is about even with the tip of the nose.

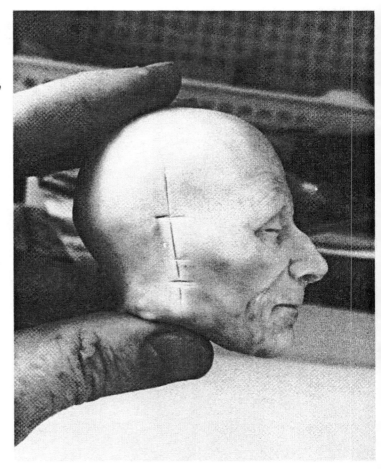

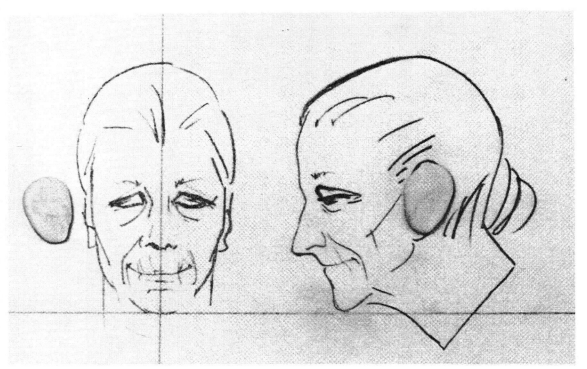

figure 33: Roughly shape two pats of Sculpey into ovals. Check with the diagram for size. Keep them thin, about 1/16".

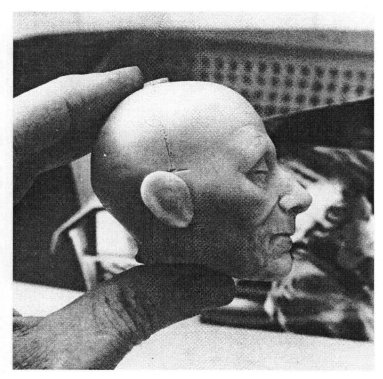

figure 34: Place the ear shapes on their respective ear placement lines.

figure 35: Press firmly on the front edge of each ear.

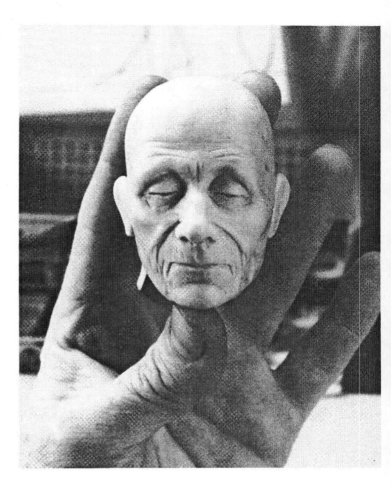

figure 36: Leave each ear free from the head at the top, bottom and back.

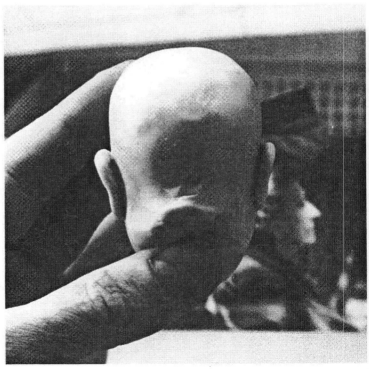

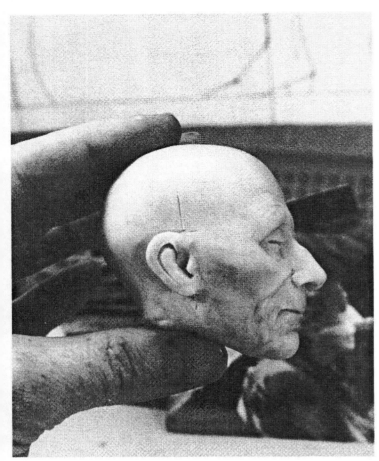

figure 37: Smooth the pieces into the head at the front. Use the tool to draw in the inner lines of each ear, roughly shaped like a reversed "S". Push the tool in about 1/4" to form the earhole. Smooth by pressing around the edges of the earhole.

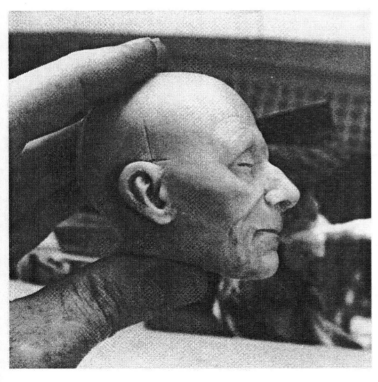

figure 38: Continue to refine the ear. Pad the lobe if necessary. (The best way to sculpt an ear is to find someone to model for you.)

figure 39: Form the bowl of each ear by placing rolls of Sculpey behind the shell and blending.

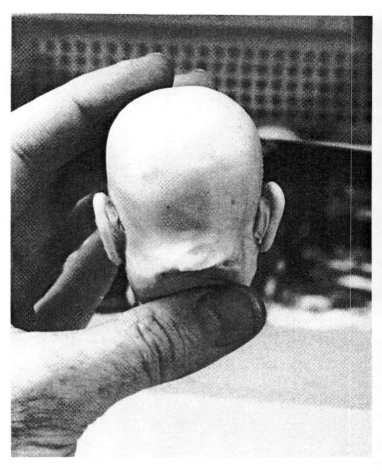

figure 40: With the ears in place, shaped and blended, the head is essentially finished. Smooth as much as you like, add wrinkle detail, and refine to your heart's content. Gently wrap in paper towels and place in the refrigerator until time to attach the shoulder plate.

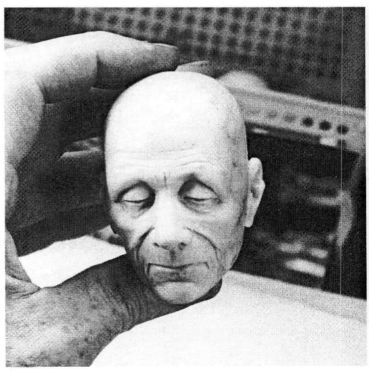

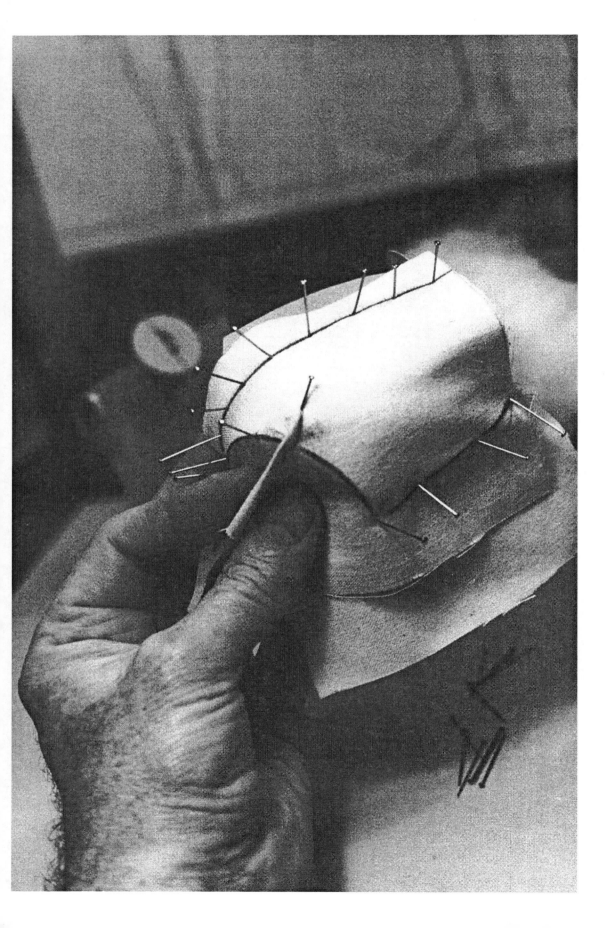

Developing the Body Pattern

4

The following method of draping unbleached muslin over a cardboard armature lightly padded with Fiberfil will give an accurate pattern from which a doll's actual body may be cut, sewn and stuffed. This method of making a doll body may appear a bit tricky but really isn't as complicated nor as time consuming as you may first think.

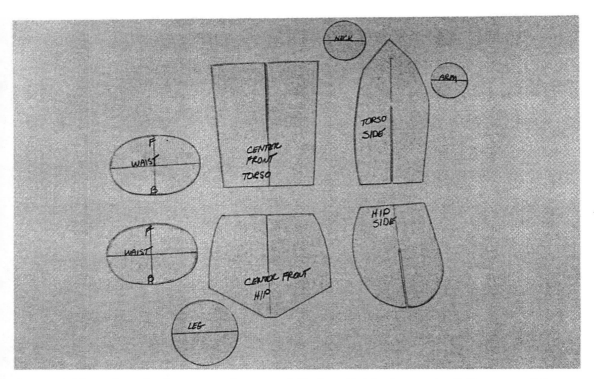

figure 1: To make a body pattern for your doll, first divide the original diagram of the doll's body into sections on a piece of tracing paper. On the front view trace a straight line down the side from the high point of the shoulder to the waist and a straight line down from the neck through the crotch, dividing the torso in half. Draw a line perpendicular from the high point of the shoulder and at right angles to the center front line. Draw a line at the waist from the side through and at right angles to the center front line. Do the same at the crotch. Draw a line at about a 45 degree angle where the leg will join the hip to the center front line. (Imagine a panty line.) You will need a circle with the diameter of that measurement. Trace the side view of the torso and hip. Divide it at the waist. Draw a straight line down from the high point of the center back neck to the waist, dividing the waist exactly in half. The length of this line should equal the side seam measurement on the front view. It does not go all the way to the center back neck. Divide the hip in half at the waist down to the crotch. The length of this line should equal the center front line on the front view. Using the measurement of the waist from side seam to side seam and from front to back, draw an oval leaving the lines as guide lines and dividing it in half side to side and front to back. Measure the width of the neck. Using that measurement as the diameter, draw a circle. Do the same for the arm where it will join the torso. Transfer the pattern pieces to a piece of cardboard about the weight and thickness of the back of a legal pad or cereal box. Cut the pieces out. Cut halfway down the center front line from the shoulder on the front view. Cut halfway up from the waist on the center dividing line of the side view. Go back and make another cut beside the first cut to widen it and compensate for the thickness of the cardboard. Do the same thing with the hips—halfway down from the waist on the center front line, halfway up on the center line of the side view.

figure 2: Slide the side torso onto the front piece. Make sure the two pieces are even at the waist and that the shoulder line meets the center of the side piece. If the pieces do not fit exactly, then trim them at the waist. Glue the pieces together where they intersect. Elmer's glue will work fine, but hot melt glue is much faster. Glue the waist oval to the torso using the guide lines to hold the front and side torso pieces at right angles to one another. Cut four pegs from balsa wood and glue them to the side piece at the neck and the front piece at the arm. This will help hold the circles at right angles to the torso pieces.

figure 3: This is the finished armature or form on which the muslin will be draped to achieve the pattern for the cut and sewn body. It isn't pretty, but it doesn't have to be.

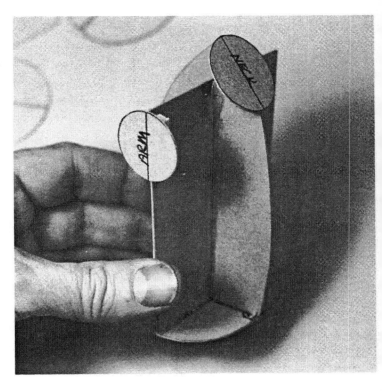

figure 4: The procedure is the same for the hip section. Slide the side hip onto the front and glue. Glue the oval piece at the waist and glue two balsa wood pegs where the leg will join the hips.

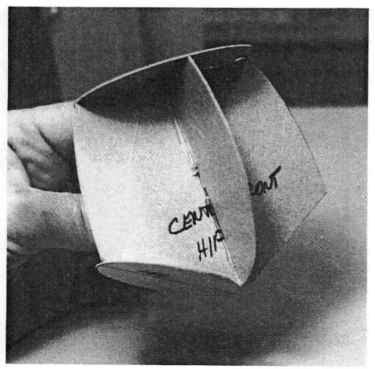

figure 5: Glue the circle to the pegs, and the hip form is ready to be draped.

figure 6: Hold the two body sections together. Make sure the waist ovals are the same size and shape. If they are not, trim them to match.

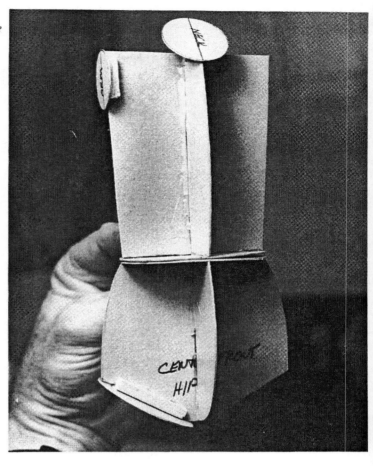

figure 7: The hip section is the easier to drape. Begin by cutting a piece of muslin long enough to reach from the center front waist completely around the hip to the center back waist plus about two inches. The width should be from the center to the side plus two inches. With a ruler draw a line 1/2" from the raw edge of the muslin running the entire length of the muslin and following the grain.

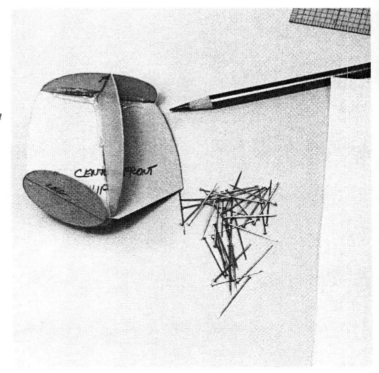

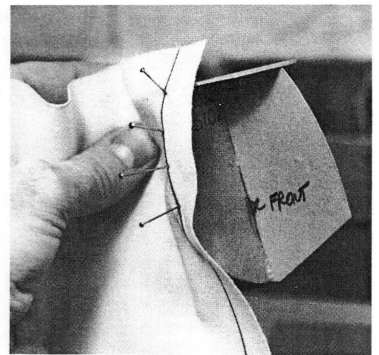

figure 8: Place the pencil line drawn on the muslin on the center of the cardboard hip section, extending an inch above the waist line. Pin it through the cardboard at the center front waist. Line up with the center front edge and pin down toward the crotch every 1/2".

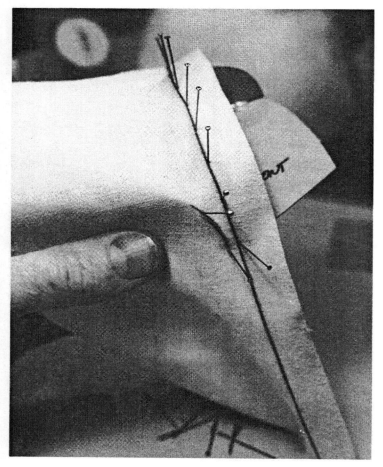

figure 9: Continue to pin the center line to the crotch. Smooth the muslin over the hip disk and pin. Mark between the pins as you go. Keep the pins 1/2" or less apart.

figure 10: Put a small piece of Fiberfil in the front section of the hip block. This will hold the muslin out and give you a round hip. Use just a small amount to pad out the shape.

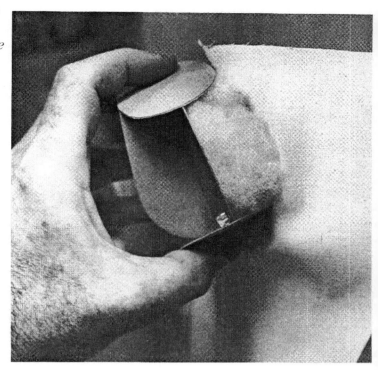

figure 11: Continue to pin around the hip disk to the side, marking as you go.

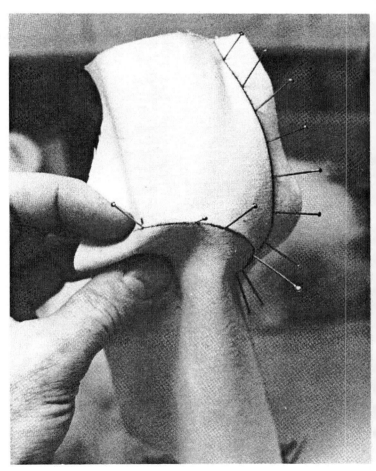

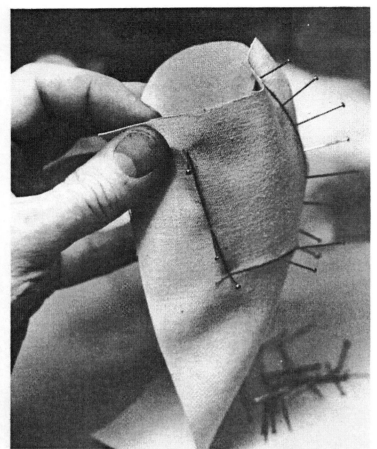

figure 12: Pin up the side of the cardboard armature making sure the grain of the muslin is remaining at right angles to the center front. Pin securely at the waist. You will notice that the muslin is larger at the waist. A dart will be taken out at the waist forming the shape of the tummy.

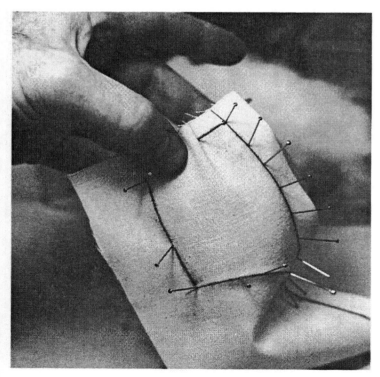

figure 13: Pin the muslin from the center front waist to about halfway the distance to the side. Gently push the muslin from the side waist toward the center front until it meets the pin marking the halfway point, and the dart will form.

figure 14: Pin and mark the dart.

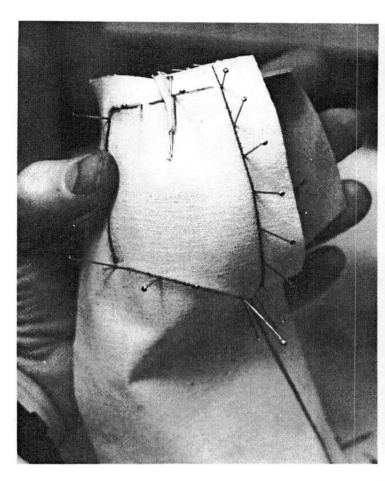

figure 15: Turn the hip over and continue pinning the center line of the muslin to the center of the cardboard hip block. Pin and mark up to the waist. Keeping the grain straight, pin around the hip disk to about halfway to the side.

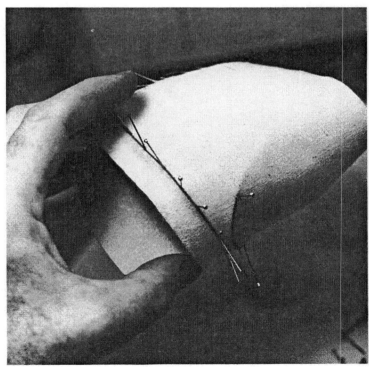

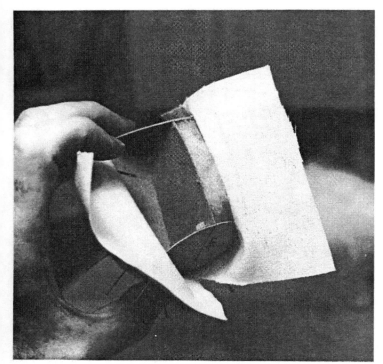

figure 16: Unpin the front from the side and push it out of the way. It may be necessary to slash the muslin at the disk area as it was done here.

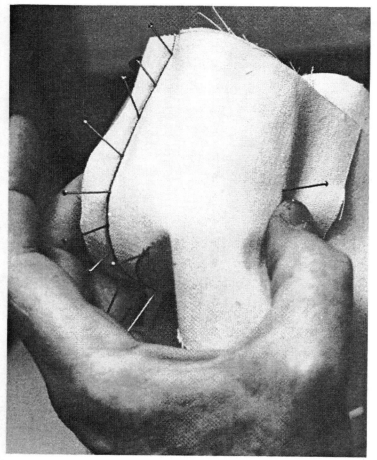

figure 17: Pad the back section with a little Fiberfil and smooth the muslin over to the side. A dart will begin to form at the hip disk which will give the buttocks their shape.

figure 18: Pin to the waist and around the hip disk. When you reach the halfway point, pin and mark the dart.

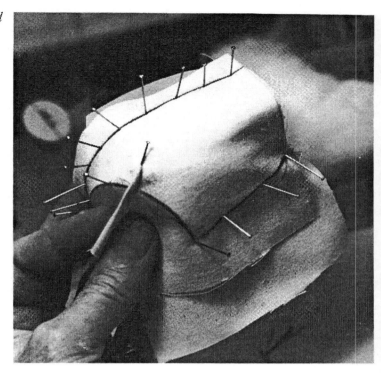

figure 19: Pin from center back to about halfway to the side seam at the waist. Then pin from the side toward the center. Pin and mark the dart that will form. This dart will not be straight but rather should be a cat's eye shape to give the buttocks their form.

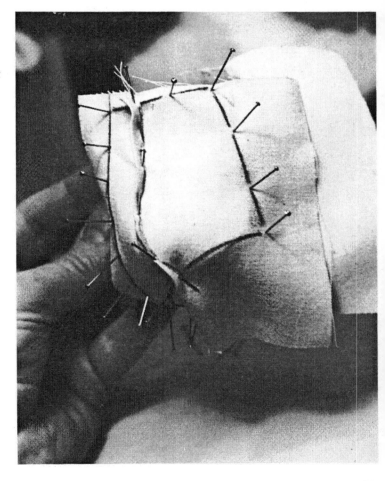

figure 20: Unpin the muslin and press it smooth. This is the complete hip pattern. The center is cut on the fold of the fabric. The pattern is in three sections with the side back joining the back with a shaped seam.

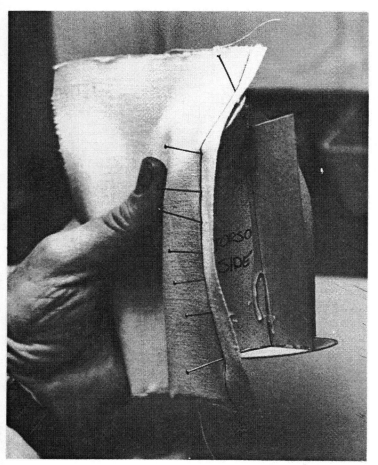

figure 21: Prepare a piece of muslin for the torso the length of the center front from the back of the neck to the waist plus two inches. Line the center of the muslin up with the center of the torso block and pin it at the center back neck and once again at the front or base of the neck and continue down to the waist.

figure 22: At the base of the neck, smooth the muslin over to the arm disk keeping the grain straight. Pin the muslin to the arm disk and mark.

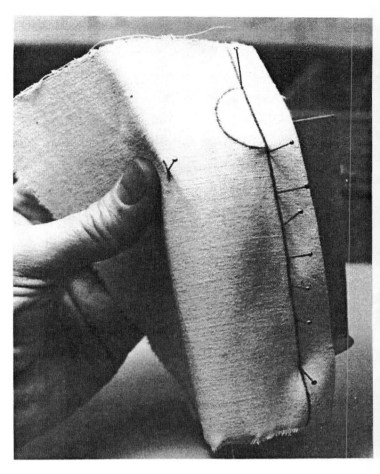

figure 23: Pin the muslin up the arm disk to the shoulder and mark. Mark the neck disk and draw a line from the center back neck to the high point of the arm disk.

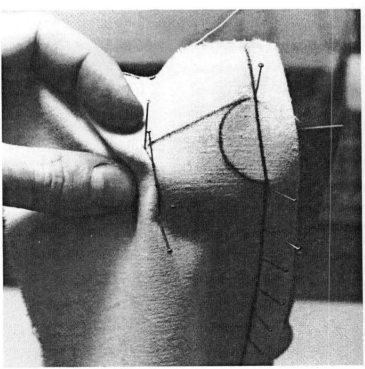

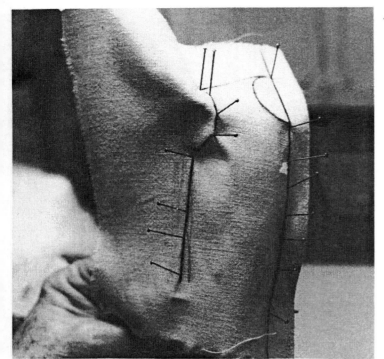

figure 24: Pad out the front section of the torso block and continue to pin the arm disk to the side and down the side to the waist.

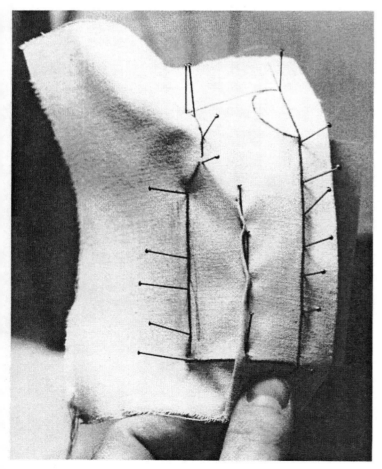

figure 25: Pin from the side to the halfway point on the waist and from the center toward the side. Pin and mark the dart that will form. The dart should end just below the arm disk.

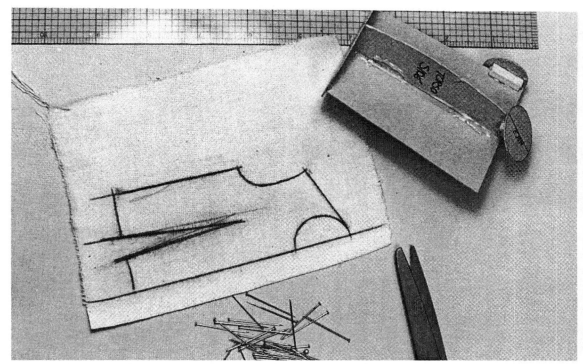

figure 26: Unpin the muslin and press. This dart seemed to point a bit too much toward the side so it was corrected with a ruler.

figure 27: Prepare a piece of muslin just as you did for the front. Pin it to the center back of the torso starting at the neck and pinning down to the waist.

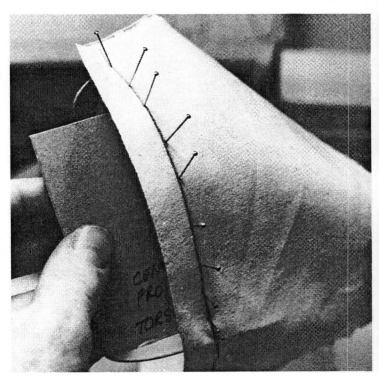

figure 28: Smooth the muslin from the center front torso armature to the arm disk, pinning and keeping the grain straight as you go. Mark and then pin the arm disk to the shoulder. Mark a straight line from the neck to the shoulder.

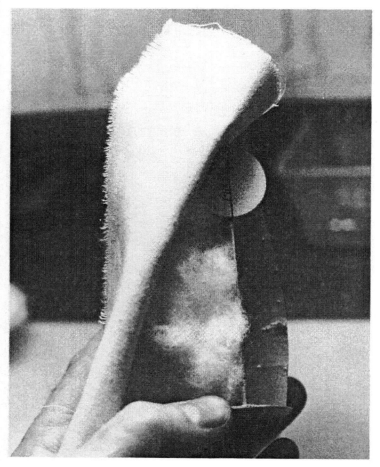

figure 29: Pad out the back section with a bit of Fiberfil—just enough to hold the muslin out.

figure 30: Pin the arm disk to the side and down the side to the waist.

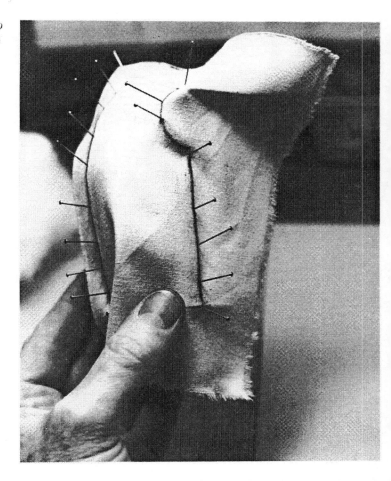

figure 31: Pin the muslin to the waist from the side and from the center, meeting in the middle of the disk. Pin and mark the dart. The center back dart is longer than the front, going beyond the armhole.

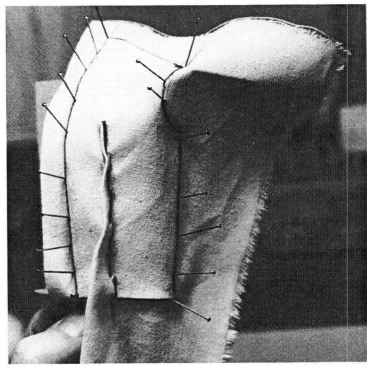

figure 32: Remove the muslin and press.

figure 33: Trace onto paper the muslin pieces using a ruler to straighten the lines. Make certain the side seams match perfectly, as well as the shoulder seams. Do not put seam allowance on the pattern.

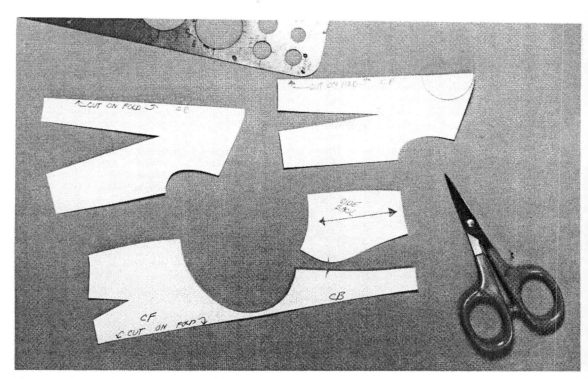

figure 34: Cut the pattern out of heavy paper such as Bristol Board. Mark the grain lines and label each piece.

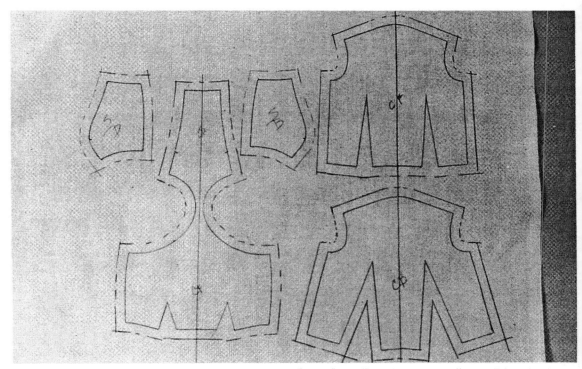

figure 35: Mark off the pattern onto a piece of good quality, heavyweight, unbleached muslin. Following the grain line, place the center fronts and center backs on the fold. Mark two side back pieces. Add 1/4" seam allowance.

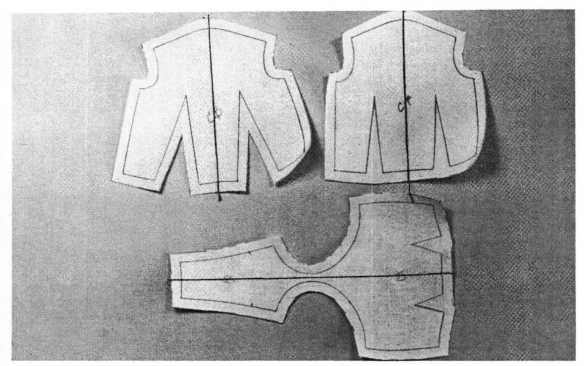

figure 36: Machine stitch the center lines of all the pieces. This stitch line is an invaluable guide line when you are joining all the pieces. Use white thread. Black was used here for reasons of photography.

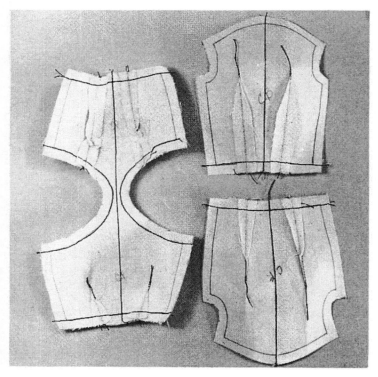

figure 37: Stitch the side back to the center back of the hip. Press the seam open, clipping at the curve. Stitch all the darts closed, slash them and press open. Stay stitch around the bottom of the hips and at the waist of both the hip pieces and the torso. Stay stitching is a machine stitch which follows the seam line keeping the fabric from stretching out of shape.

figure 38: Cut a cardboard disk the size of the doll's neck. Cut a hole in the center to accept the armature wire and glue it with white glue to the front matching the centers and touching the shoulder seam. Stitch the shoulder seam, clip the curve and press open. Stay stitch the armhole.

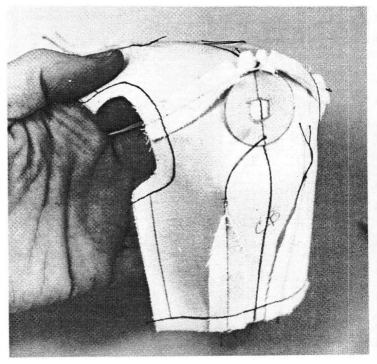

figure 39: Stitch the side seams of both pieces, press open and turn. The body is ready for the armature wire and stuffing.

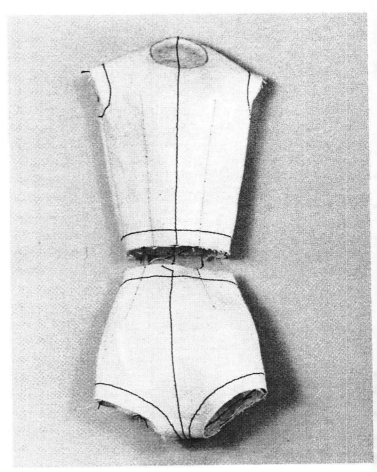

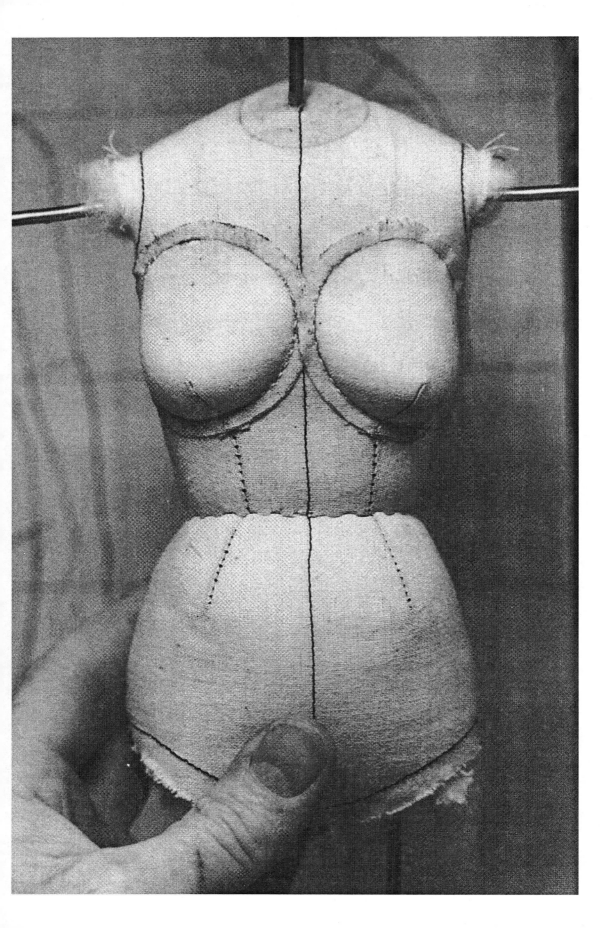

Making the Body

5

The body armature I use is the simplest one I could come up with. An armature is necessary to hold the form upright. This armature is flexible enough to be bent to the correct posture, helping the figure find its balance. You can use aluminum armature wire but I prefer #8 gauge copper wire found at electrical supply houses and at some hardware stores. Soldering is not necessary since both pieces are twisted together and bound with fine gauge wire.

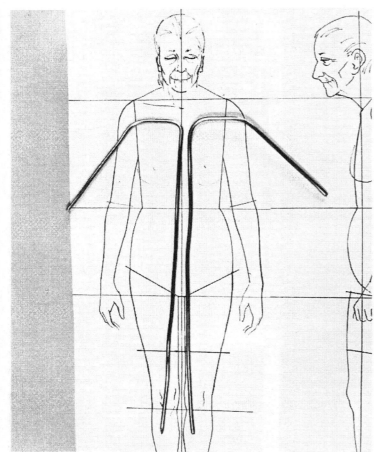

figure 1: Using the diagram as a guide, begin the body armature by cutting two pieces of wire that measure from below the elbow up to the shoulder, across the center front and down, well below the knee. Bend the wire pieces at right angles at center front to form the shoulders and arms.

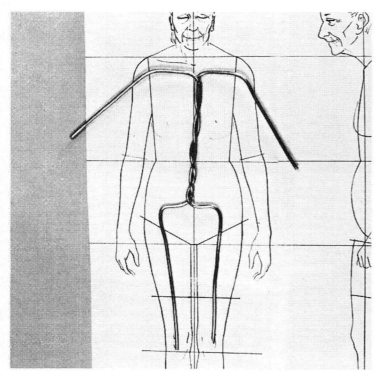

figure 2: Twist the wires together down to mid-hip length. This forms the spine. Bend the wire at right angles to form the hips and again to form the legs.

figure 3: Cut a small piece of wire about three inches long and twist it onto the top of the spine. This forms the neck.

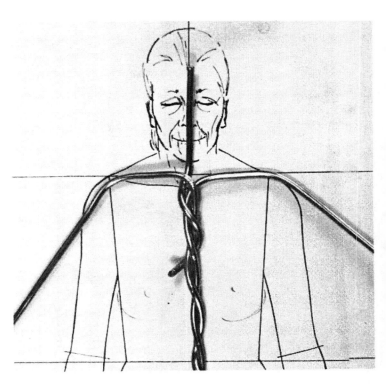

figure 4: Use a fine gauge wire and wrap the neck wire and spine together.

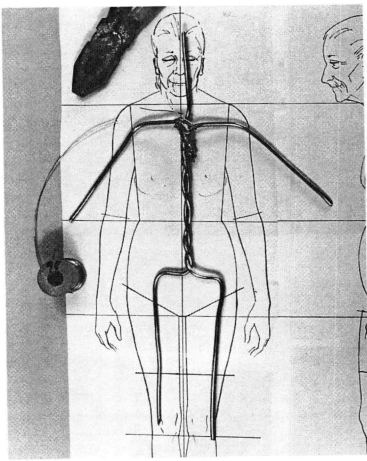

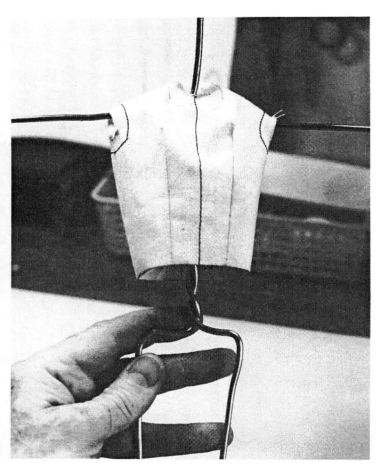

figure 5: Push the neck wire through the center of the cardboard circle glued at the neck. Bend the arm wires up and slip the torso over the armature like slipping on a T-shirt. Bend the arm wires out straight.

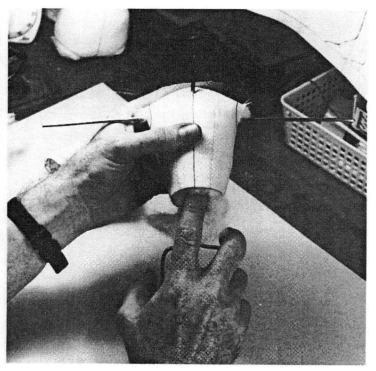

figure 6: The torso is stuffed through the waist opening. Tear small pieces of fiberfil about the size of a small lemon and push them in with your fingers. Keep the armature wire centered as you stuff. Turn the torso constantly, packing it firmly, and when you think it is filled enough, go back and do some more. It takes a surprising amount of fiberfil to make a body as firm as it should be.

figure 7: With the torso stuffed and the wire centered, turn the waist line seam allowance up at the stay stitch line.

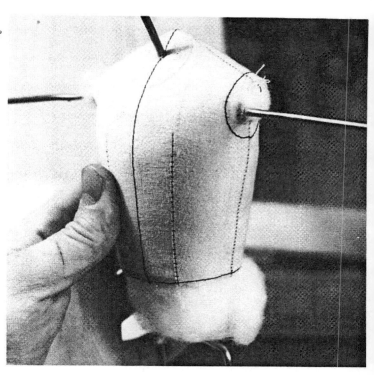

figure 8: Slide the hip piece over the armature. Pin at center front, center back, and side seams. The darts may or may not line up; it isn't necessary that they do, but the centers and sides must.

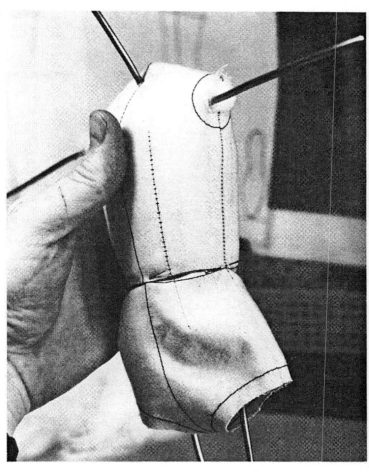

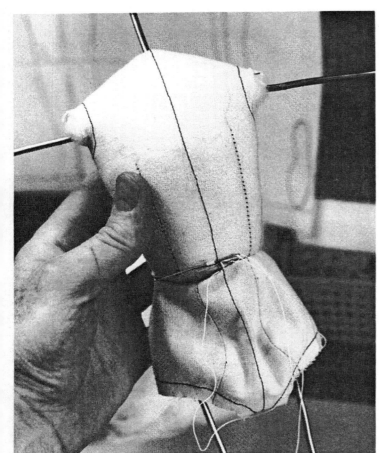

figure 9: Use a good strong thread such as four-cord thread or buttonhole twist and stitch the hips to the torso. The ladder stitch is about the only hand stitch I use except for hemming. It is easy to do and is invaluable in joining sections of the body and for costuming. The ladder stitch, so called because it resembles a ladder until it is pulled taut, is a running stitch taken on one side of the seam and then on the other. When the thread is pulled, the two sides of the seam meet with the seam allowance turned to the inside. Done carefully, it makes an invisible join.

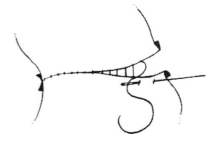

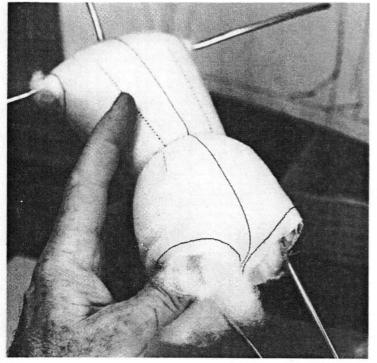

figure 10: Stuff the hips through the openings where the legs attach. Keep the wires centered and stuff firmly. The shape can be controlled somewhat with careful stuffing, but if the pattern is good, just good hard stuffing will give you an accurate form.

figure 11: The stuffed body ready for the breasts.

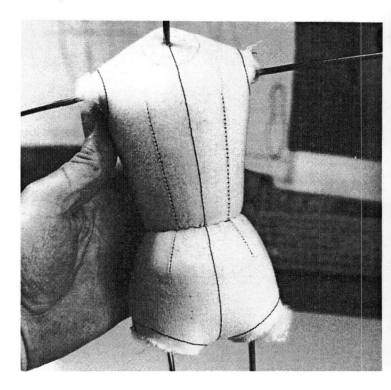

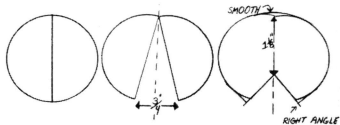

figure 12: To arrive at a pattern for the breasts, estimate the size of the breasts and draw a circle. In this case the circle has a diameter of 1 5/8". Draw a line dividing the circle exactly in half. Cut the circle out and slash through the dividing line leaving it just barely connected at the tips. Spread the circle about 3/4". The more you spread it, the larger the dart will be, hence the fuller the breast will be. Draw in a new center line. Measure down the center line to where the bust point will be. On a young figure the bust point is high, on an older figure it is lower. This bust point is 1 1/8" down the center line. Draw in the dart connecting the bust point to the bottom of the circle where it has been spread. Smooth the top of the pattern so it does not dip and make the bottom join the lines of the dart at right angles.

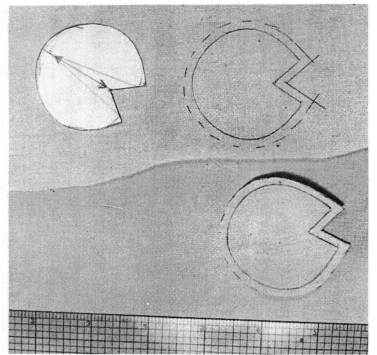

figure 13: Cut the pattern out of paper, fold out the dart and pin the pattern to the torso to check the size and the placement of the bust point. Flat pattern drafting, except in the hands of a master, is a trial and error proposition, so if the breast is too big or too small, have another go at it. This particular pattern required two attempts before I was satisfied. Mark the pattern onto muslin, the center line on the straight grain. Add 1/4" seam allowance and cut out.

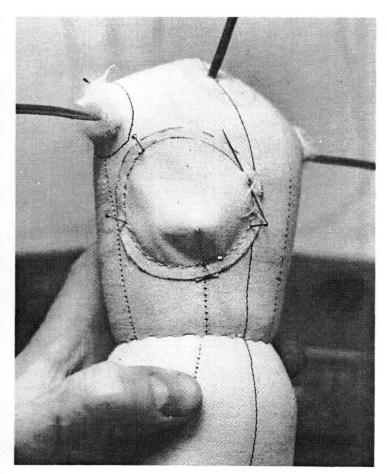

figure 14: Stitch the dart closed and press. Pin the breast piece in place and stitch using a short running stitch. There is no need to turn the seam allowance under unless you particularly want to—I seldom do. Leave an opening in the top for stuffing.

figure 15: A small hemostat is almost a necessity in stuffing the breasts. Use small pieces of fiberfil. Pack the fiberfil very firmly at the bottom, but as you work up past the bust point, begin to pad just slightly, allowing the top of the breast to join the torso smoothly with no sudden bump.

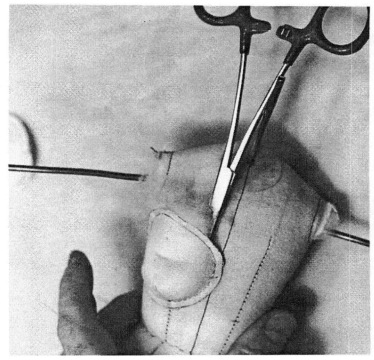

figure 16: The finished torso with both breasts in place. The next step is the making of the shoulder plate.

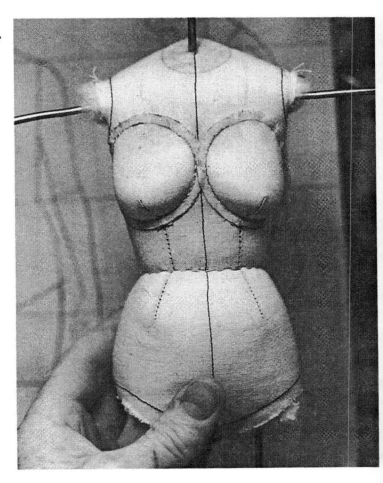

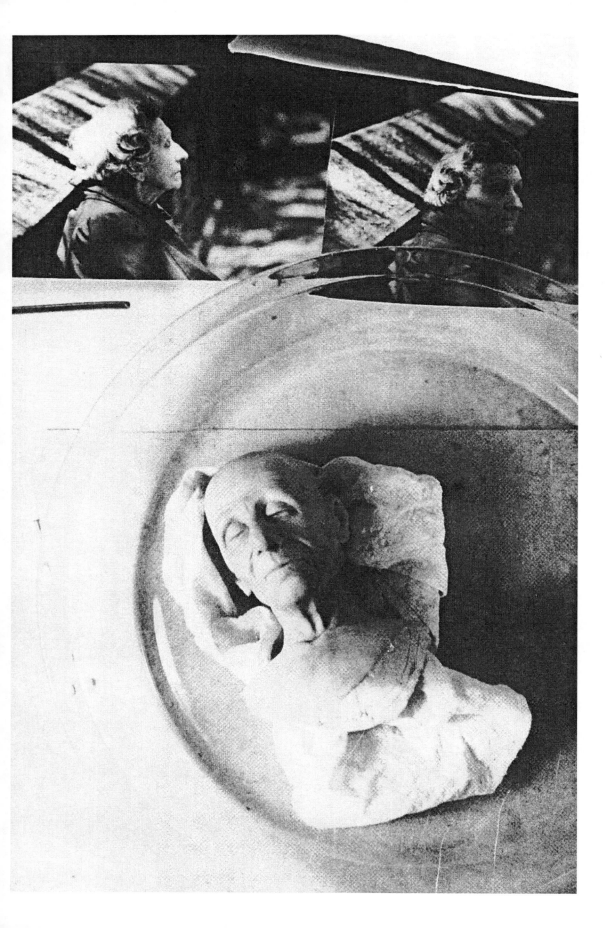

The Shoulder Plate

6

The shoulder plate supports the head and finishes off the exposed part of the torso. The shape is arbitrary and depends on the neckline of the costume and how much of the upper torso will be left uncovered. The method of making a shoulder plate that I use, except for drying time, is fast and easy to do. It ensures an exact fit and does not show under the snuggest costume. Using the torso pattern made in the chapter "Developing the Body Pattern", place the shoulder seams of the pattern together, center back to center front, with the tops of the armholes matching. Measure down for the neck on the center back line about 1 1/2". Draw a curved line from that mark to the top of the armhole where it meets the shoulder line. Measure down the center front line about three inches and draw a curved line from that point to the top of the armhole. Place the center front line on the fold and cut out what is now the shoulder plate pattern. The center back line will form a deep dart which will shape the shoulder plate to fit the torso exactly.

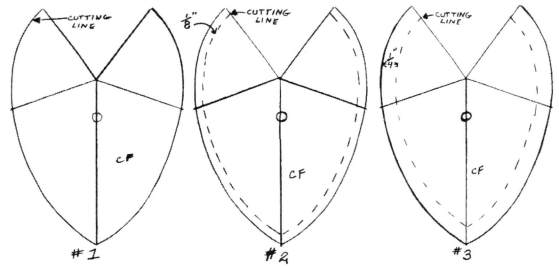

figure 1: Mark off the pattern for the shoulder plate on three pieces of muslin and mark them #1, #2, and #3. Cut out piece #1 the same size as the pattern. The outer edge of piece #2 should be marked and cut an eighth of an inch inside the outer edge of the pattern making a smaller piece. The outer edge of piece #3 should be marked and cut a quarter of an inch inside the pattern's outer edge. This procedure staggers the outer edge of the plate causing it to fit smoothly with no ridge to show under the costume. The dart on the pattern should be marked on all three pieces and cut out. Be sure to cut a small hole at the center front of each piece to accept the neck wire.

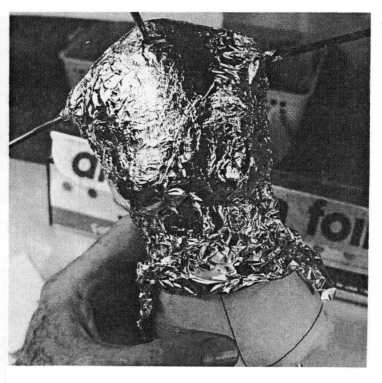

figure 2: Cover the torso with a piece of aluminum foil, pressing it tightly to the muslin. Pin it in place if necessary.

figure 3: Take piece #3, which is the smallest, and give the wrong side a good thick coat of Elmer's glue. Elmer's is a hard glue and dries very stiff making the shoulder plate rigid.

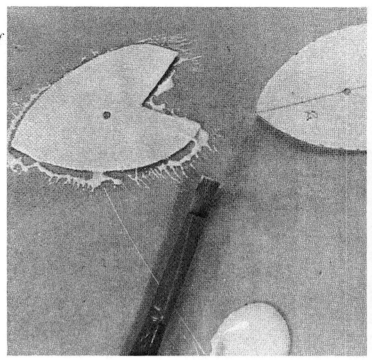

figure 4: Push the neck wire through the hole of the muslin piece and press the muslin piece firmly and smoothly to the foil covered torso. Be sure to line up the center front of the muslin piece to the center front of the torso.

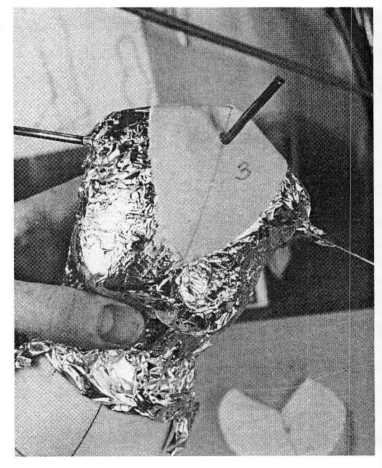

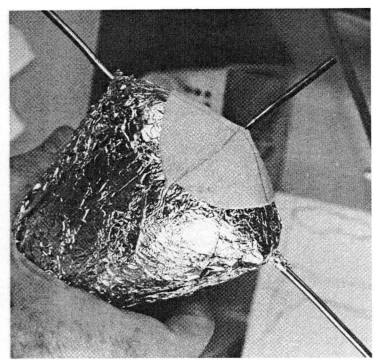

figure 5: Close the center back dart by butting the two edges of the dart together. Use your finger to smooth the muslin to the foil.

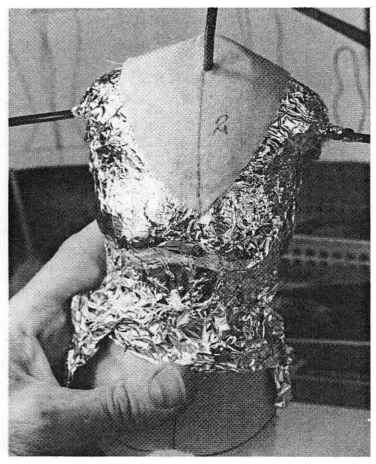

figure 6: Repeat the last two steps with muslin piece #2, gluing it on top of piece #3. Smooth it carefully removing air bubbles.

figure 7: Glue piece #1, which is the largest piece, to piece #2 as in the last step. Set the torso aside to dry overnight.

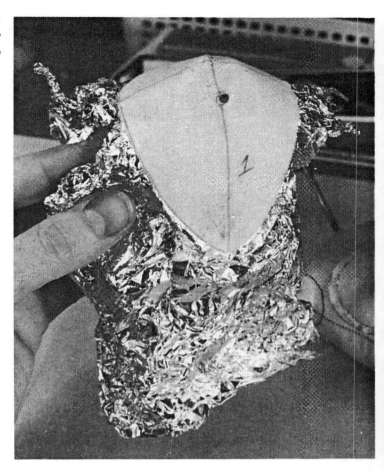

figure 8: When the plate is dry, carefully pull the foil off the torso. The plate will stick to the foil, but it can be peeled off easily. Trim the edges if necessary.

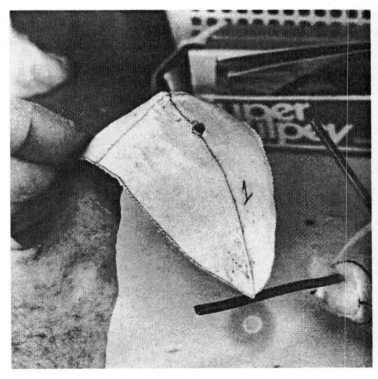

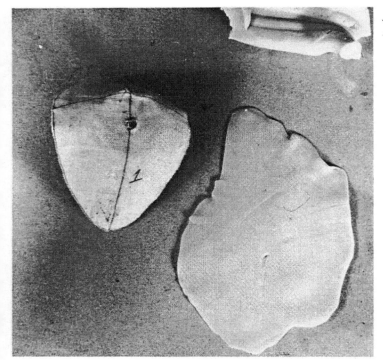

figure 9: Flatten out a thin piece of Sculpey large enough to cover the shoulder plate. Make it as thin as you can. This layer of Sculpey is the top surface or "skin" of the shoulder plate.

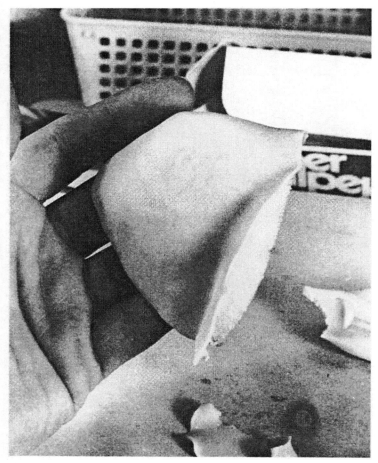

figure 10: Place the Sculpey pancake over the muslin shoulder plate and press firmly. Smooth it from the center to the outer edges. Pull any excess off the edges. Be very careful to press out any air bubbles that may form.

figure 11: Place the Sculpey covered shoulder plate on the torso. Mark the neck circle lightly with the tool. Indicate the center front line and the shoulder blades. Pin it in place.

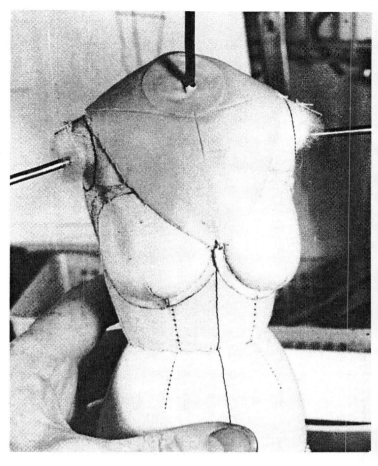

figure 12: Roll a piece of Sculpey to the size of the neck circle. Measure the diagram for the length and cut it to that measurement. Push the neck down onto the neck wire to the shoulder plate. Press it firmly in place and smooth into the plate.

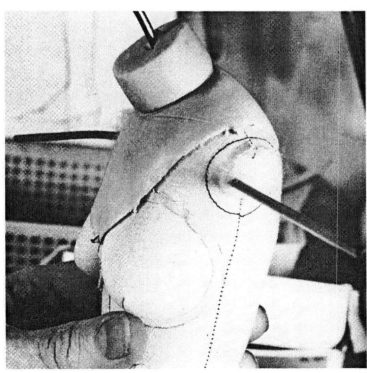

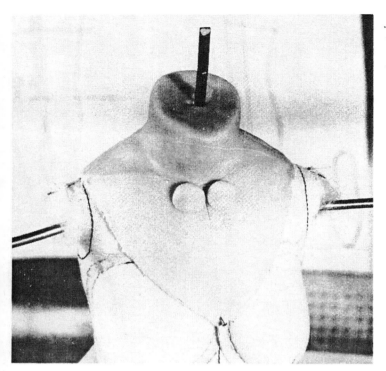

figure 13: Roll two pellets of Sculpey, each about the size of a pea, and press one on either side of the center front line at the base of the neck.

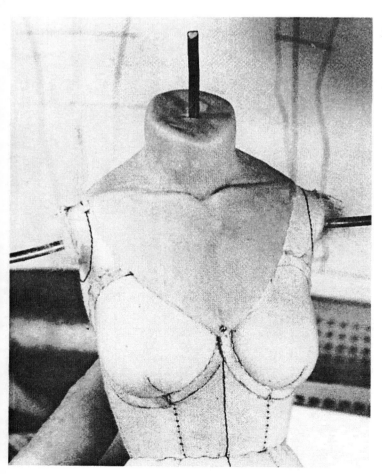

figure 14: Smooth these pellets into the plate from the center toward the shoulder lines where they meet the armholes. These form the shoulder blades.

figure 15: With the neck attached to the shoulder plate, the head can now be removed from its protective wrapping and pushed down on the wire until it meets the neck. It may be necessary to clip the wire a bit shorter to avoid hitting the foil ball inside the head. Check to be sure the neck is the correct length by measuring the diagram. Pose the head as you wish; this doll is looking down, so the neck is a bit shorter in the front.

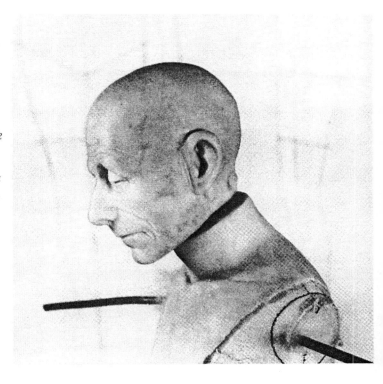

figure 16: Smooth and blend the neck into the head. Fill any gaps (usually at the back) with pieces of Sculpey. Make this good and strong, as well as smooth. Blend the neck all the way around, under the chin and up the back behind the jaw line.

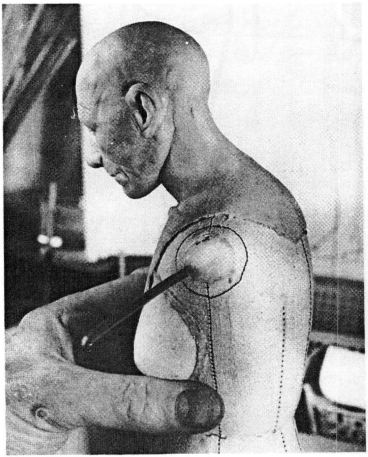

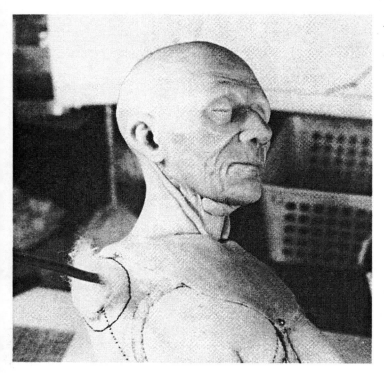

*figure 17: Roll coils of Sculpey
and place them on the neck
just behind each ear down to
the center front. Pad the area
under the chin where the flesh
has sagged.*

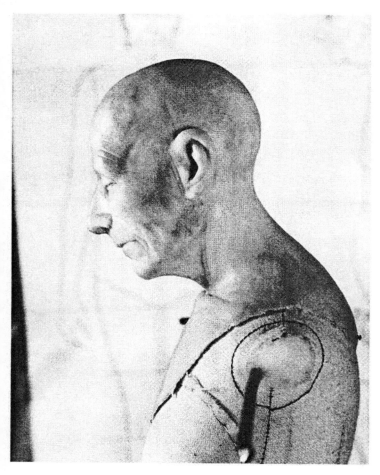

*figure 18: Blend and smooth
the coils and pads into the
neck and head. Add any detail
and wrinkles you wish at this
point. When the sculpture is
where you want it, smooth the
surface with a brush and
acetone or lacquer thinner.
(Remember to avoid breathing
these or any other solvents or
having them in prolonged
contact with your skin.)*

figure 19: Very carefully pull the head and shoulder plate off the torso. Check out the sculpture and surface. Make sure they are the way you want them. If they are, the head and shoulder plate can be cured.

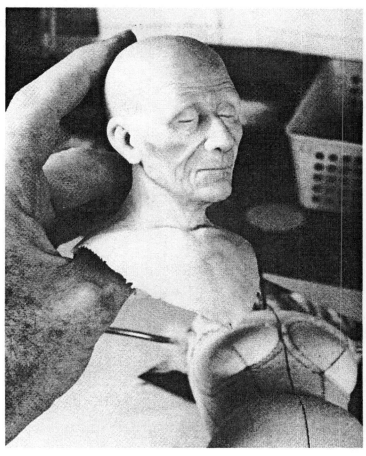

figure 20: Follow the instructions on the box of Sculpey and preheat the oven to 300°. Make a cushion of paper towels in a pie plate. Lay the head face up on the towels and place in the oven. Super Sculpey cures in fifteen to twenty minutes. The head and shoulder plate will be attached to the body after they are painted and the body is given its final touches in the chapter entitled "Character Padding".

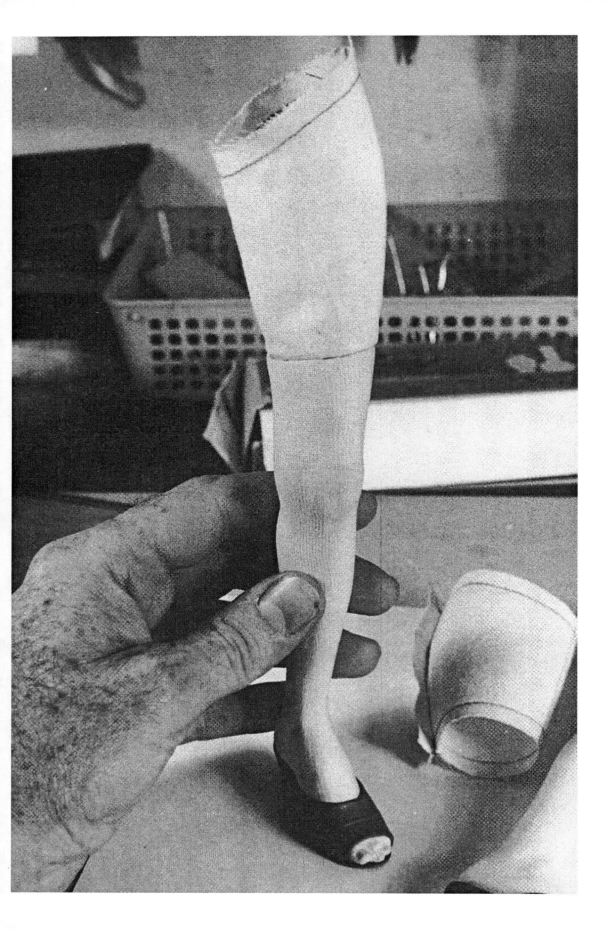

Legs, Feet, Hose and Shoes

7

A cardboard armature is made for each leg the same way that one is made for the body pattern. The only difference is that each leg is actually sculpted onto its cardboard armature with the cardboard remaining inside the leg. Shoes and hose are made and glued onto the feet and legs before the legs are attached to the rest of the body. Shoes are really not difficult to make. The degree of their success depends on the correctness of the sculpted foot and the accuracy of the pattern draping for the shoe.

However, in dollmaking one of the cardinal rules is that SOMETHING ALWAYS GOES WRONG. Mistakes and errors in judgment happen. There is always an option, however. You can live with the mistakes or you can correct them. The feet for this doll when I first made them bothered me. They seemed too small—not a lot, but enough to seem wrong. I could live with this and perhaps call the piece "Old Lady with Small Feet", or I could correct the feet. One of the really marvelous things about Sculpey is that it can be added onto and re-sculpted at any time, and so included in this chapter is an explanation of how I was able to save the original pair of legs and feet sculpted for this doll and still be able to get a final result that I found very satisfactory.

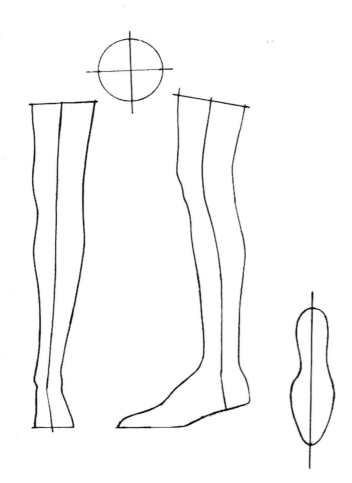

figure 1: Make cardboard armatures for legs and feet by first making tracings from the original diagram of the front and side views of one of the legs up to approximately mid-thigh. Then trace the sole of one of the feet. Make a circle the circumference of the top of a thigh based on the diameters of the front and side views. Mark these tracings off on cardboard, and flip them over so you have a right and left leg and a right and left sole. Draw a line through the center of all views of the legs from thigh to foot. These lines will curve to conform to the shape of the leg—especially if the leg is bent from the side view, as this one is.

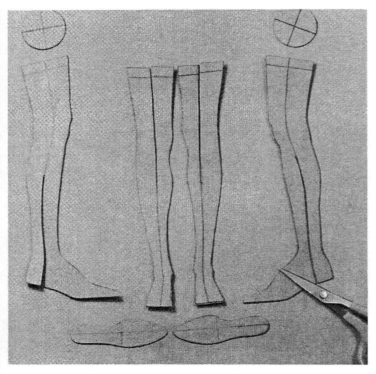

figure 2: Cut out the cardboard tracings being sure to also cut the center line of each tracing from the top of the front view of each foot down midway and from the bottom of each side view up midway. Go back and widen each slash to compensate for the thickness of the cardboard. Mark the centers of the circles with two intersecting lines. Mark the centers of the soles. Measure and draw a line 1/4" from and parallel to the top of the thigh.

figure 3: Slide the two pieces of each leg together. Line up the top edges, and the knees and ankles will line up correctly. Bend the cardboard to conform to the curved center lines. Make sure you have a left and a right leg. Line up the centers of each view at the top of each leg and glue the pieces together. Glue the circles on the tops of the legs making sure that the leg forms match the intersecting lines drawn on the circles. Glue the soles to the bottoms of the feet—left sole to left foot, right sole to right foot. (I can't tell you how many times I have glued the wrong sole to the wrong leg. This gives you a very strange leg.)

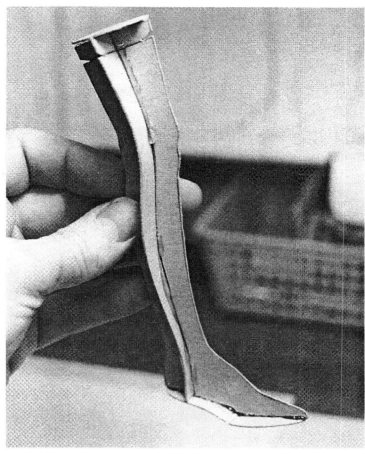

figure 4: Sometimes the front view of each leg will be longer and wider than the side view and sole.

figure 5: It may be necessary to trim the front view to fit the sole.

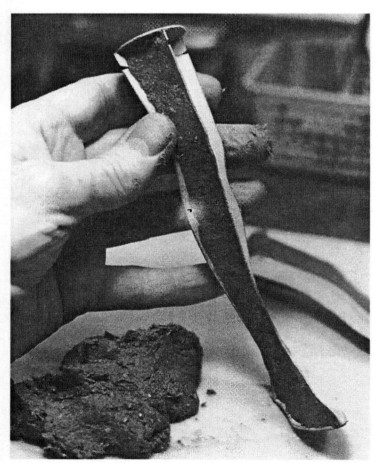

figure 6: Sculpey is wonderful stuff, but it has little tensile strength and will snap in two at points of stress. On a standing figure the legs may support the doll, but the ankles, being thin, will be weak. I reinforce each leg armature with a core of paper maché. The brand I use is Celuclay. It is very hard, strong, and lightweight. The only drawback I have found is the length of drying time—one to two days depending on the thickness. This can be speeded up in a warm oven, but it will still be about twelve hours. To use Celuclay, mix according to the package directions and fill in each section of the legs. Start at the tops and work down to the feet. Pack it in firmly up to about 1/6" from the edges.

figure 7: A layer of Sculpey goes over the Celuclay cores. Celuclay, when dry, is very porous, so while raw Sculpey will adhere to Celuclay, it tends to pull away from it once it is cured. Therefore, the Celuclay cores must be sealed. One or two coats of acrylic varnish or Elmer's glue will do the trick.

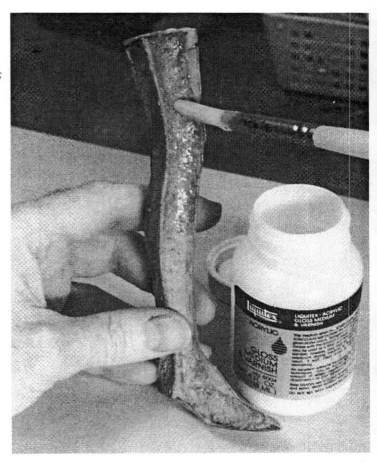

figure 8: When the sealed cores are completely dry, begin layering over each with pieces of Sculpey. Start at the top and press the Sculpey to the cores. Bring each Sculpey layer all the way out to the edges of the armatures. Think round. Do not make the layers flat from edge to edge.

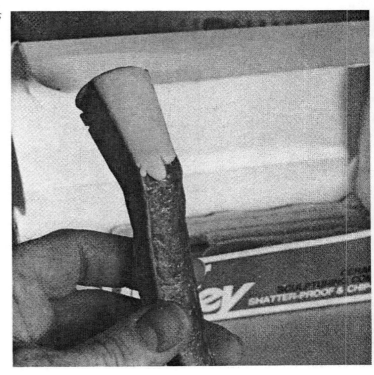

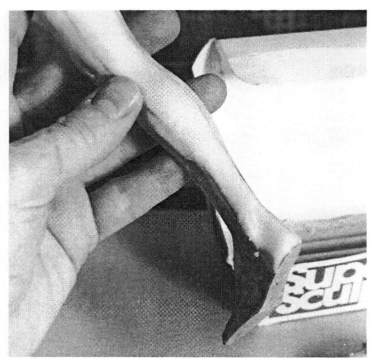

figure 9: As you go from the top down, you can add such detail as the ankles and knees. The armature will give you the correct placement for these.

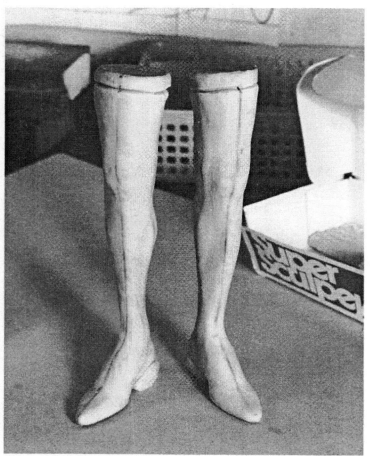

figure 10: The edges of the armatures will show through the Sculpey but will disappear when the legs are painted. When all the sections of the legs are filled in and the detail is as you want it, take the knife edge of the tool and put a groove all around the top of each thigh where the notches on the armature are. These grooves are where you will attach the muslin thighs later. With two small pellets of Sculpey make two temporary heels and stand the legs up. They should balance. If the feet are not flat on the ground, you can add a very thin layer of Sculpey to the bottom(s) to correct the balance.

figure 11: When the legs are sculpted to your satisfaction, cure them in the oven at 300° for fifteen to twenty minutes. After they have cooled you can correct any flaws with an X-acto knife, getting rid of any unwanted lumps and dimples. Other imperfections and rough places can be smoothed with a patch of spackle paste and sandpaper. Sand the leg surfaces until they are as smooth as you can get them.

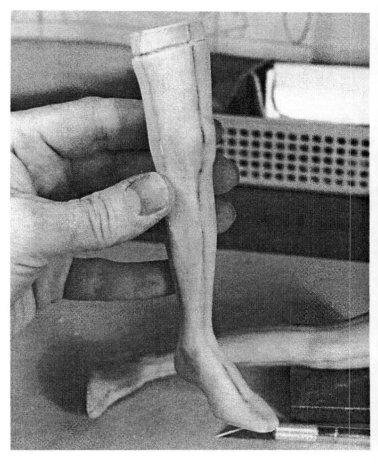

figure 12: Give the sanded legs about three coats of gesso. Sand with very fine sandpaper between each coat of gesso. The surface should be opaque white and very smooth. Give the finished legs as many coats of flesh colored paint as necessary to get a really opaque finish. (See chapter on painting the head.) You can sand lightly between each coat if you wish. I don't because I like brush strokes.

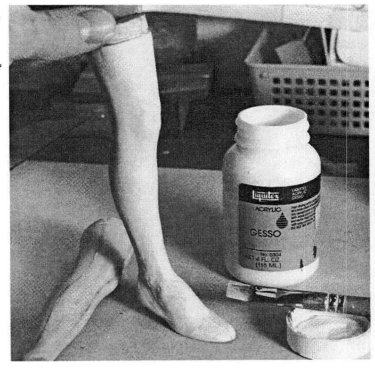

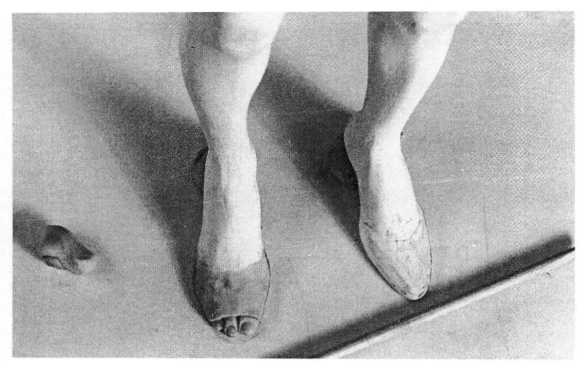

figure 13: As mentioned in the introduction to this chapter, these feet bothered me. Due to the properties of Sculpey, the correction was simple. I cut off the end of each foot and re-sculpted it, adding a bit of width and length, and I sculpted toes so my little lady could wear open-toed slippers. The difference in the size was slight...about 1/16" overall width and 1/16" length, but to my eye the feet were in better proportion.

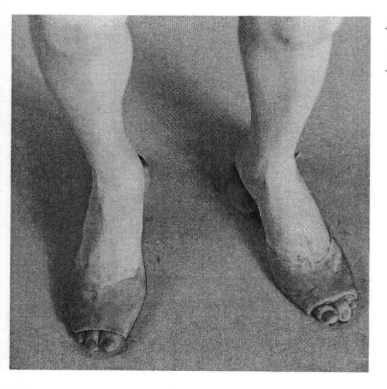

figure 14: This photograph shows the corrected feet, re-cured and repainted, ready for stockings and shoes.

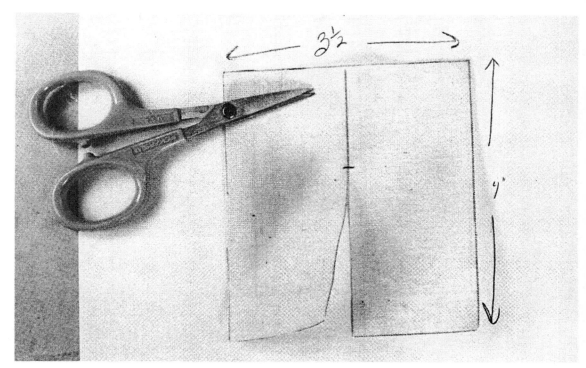

figure 15: To make shoes cut out a piece of muslin about 3 1/2" X 4". Draw a straight line through the center and slash about 2/3 of the length of that line.

figure 16: Line up the muslin on the foot, placing the center line at the center of the foot. The end of the slash should be placed where the top opening of the shoe will be. Pull the muslin under the toe and pin it securely to the cured foot. Pull the muslin back tightly and pin it behind the heel. Pull it under the foot and pin it securely.

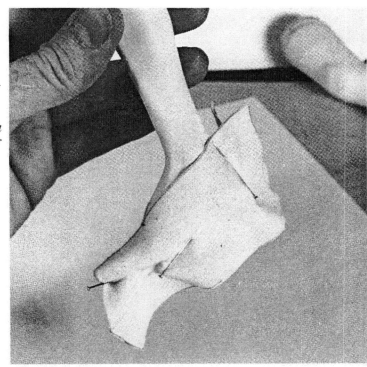

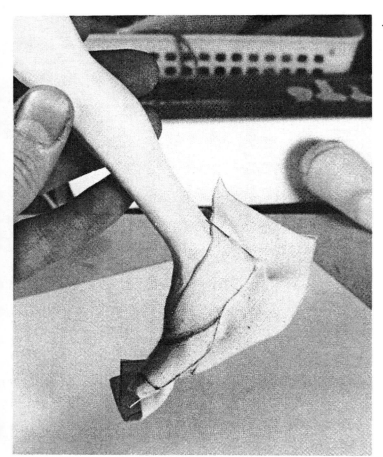

figure 17: Carefully mark around the bottom edge of the foot. Draw in the style lines of the shoe on the top of the foot.

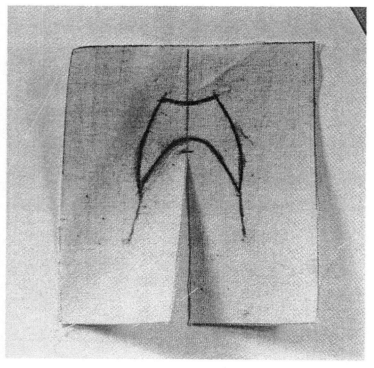

figure 18: Remove the muslin from the foot and press. Clean up the lines, and there is the pattern. The upper part of a shoe is really almost symmetrical. It is the shape of the sole that dictates if a shoe is a left or a right shoe.

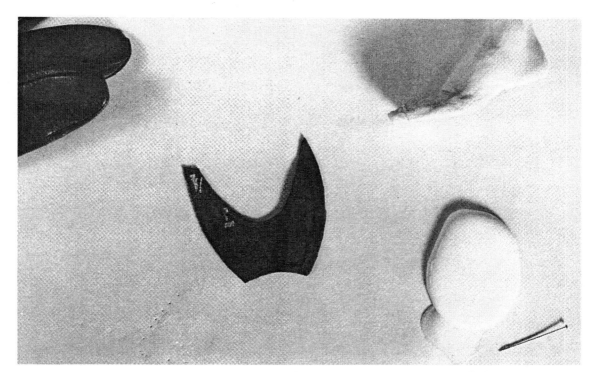

figure 19: Most of the shoes on my dolls are leather, made from used kid gloves picked up at thrift shops and flea markets. Mark off the pattern on the wrong side of the leather. Add 1/4" seam allowance along the edge that will turn under the foot to join the sole and 1/16" seam allowance at the top and the toe.

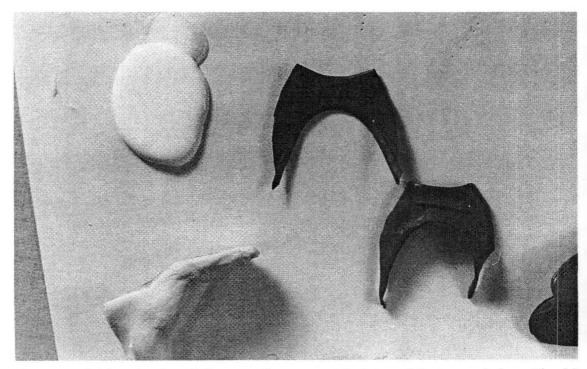

figure 20: Fold under the 1/16" seam allowance at the top and the toe and glue with white glue. Set aside to dry.

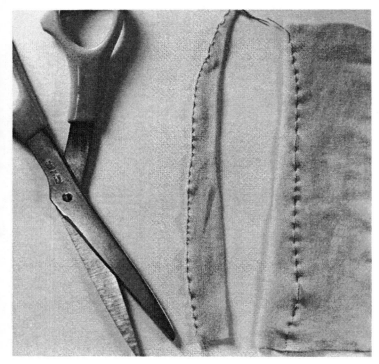

figure 21: The doll's hose are cut from nylon stockings. They are nothing more than a long tapering tube cut slightly longer than the length of the leg and small enough at the top of the leg to fit snugly. Using the closest matching thread you can find, stretch the nylon slightly as you sew. Trim the seam as close to the stitch line as you can and turn the tubes.

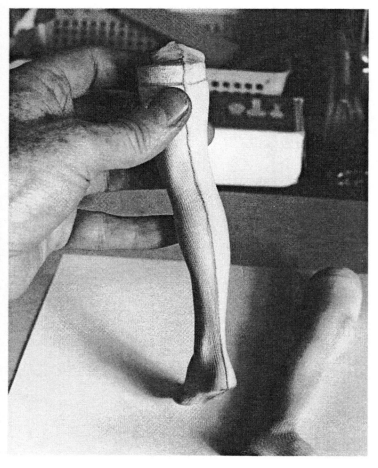

figure 22: Carefully pull the hose on the leg. Smooth them up over the top of the leg. Keep the back seam straight. Pull the toe of the hose under the foot and fasten with glue. Pull the hose over the top of the leg and glue. Once the glue has dried, trim off the excess.

figure 23: Put glue on the seam allowance of the shoe.

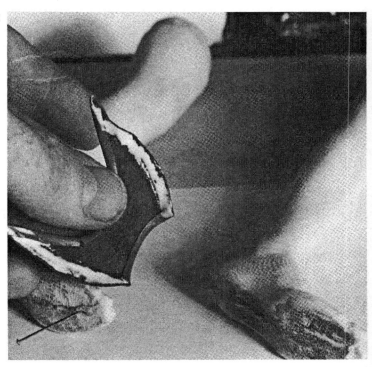

figure 24: Place the shoe over the foot and glue the sides to the bottom of the foot. Leather is very supple. It can be stretched and eased to give a very smooth, tight fitting shoe.

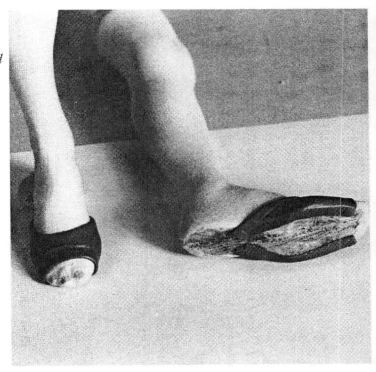

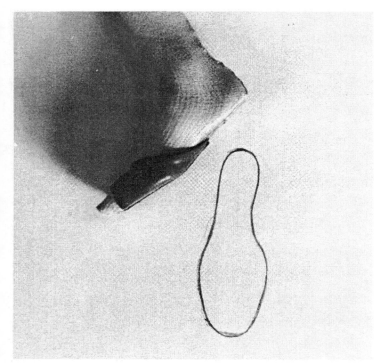

figure 25: Hold down the foot firmly on a piece of paper. (The heel will not touch.) Mark around the front of the foot. Lower the heel to touch the paper and continue to trace around the foot to get the shape of the sole. Since the two feet will not be absolutely identical, it is necessary to trace each sole separately.

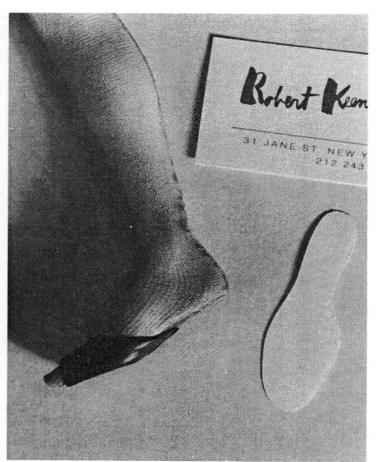

figure 26: Using the sole tracings as patterns, mark the soles off on a piece of thin cardboard (a business card is perfect) and cut out.

figure 27: Put dots of glue at the toes, the insteps, and the heels of the cardboard soles and place them on the bottoms of the feet. This is only temporary. The glue should just hold the soles in place and will be removed later.

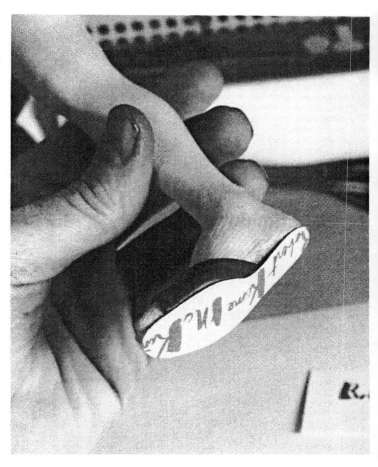

figure 28: Roll out two pieces of Sculpey long enough to cover the back part of each foot and a bit thicker than the heels will be. Firmly press each foot into a Sculpey piece, keeping the front part of each foot absolutely flat to the ground. Pull away the excess but make sure there are no gaps between each sole and where the heel will be. Carefully remove each foot and cure in the oven.

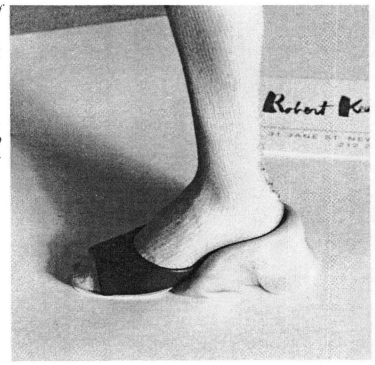

figure 29: Use an X-acto knife with a #11 blade and begin to carve the shape of each heel.

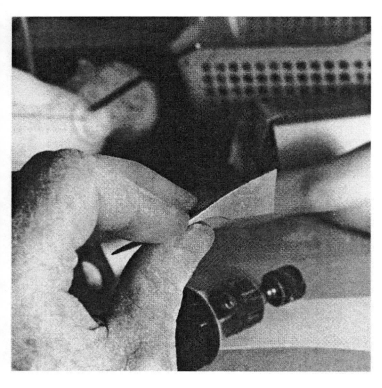

figure 30: Constantly check that the heels fit the soles. Finish shaping with sandpaper or a Dremel moto tool with a sanding drum. Glue the finished heels to the soles.

figure 31: Cut a piece of leather large enough to completely cover each sole with its attached heel.

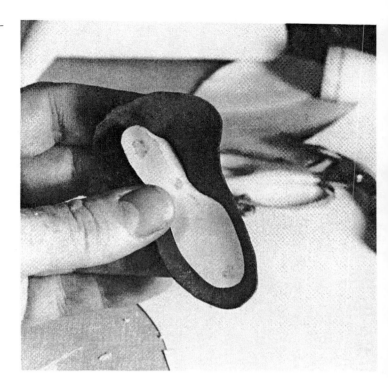

figure 32: Coat the wrong side of the leather pieces with glue and attach them to the heels and soles pulling and smoothing out all wrinkles. Trim away the excess leaving about 1/4" to glue to the top of the soles.

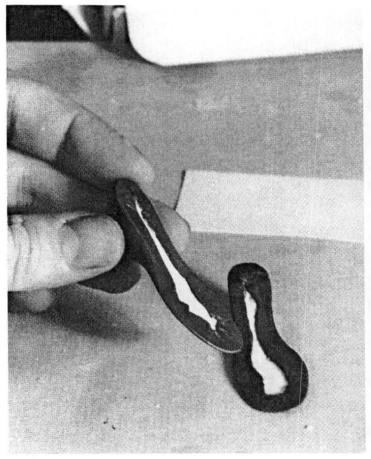

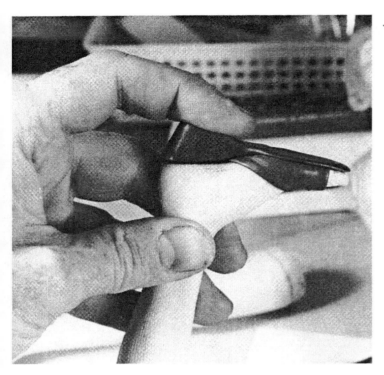

figure 33: Use 5-minute epoxy and glue the leather covered heel and sole to the bottom of the foot.

figure 34: A hole must be drilled up through each heel and into the leg and ankle about one to 1 1/2".

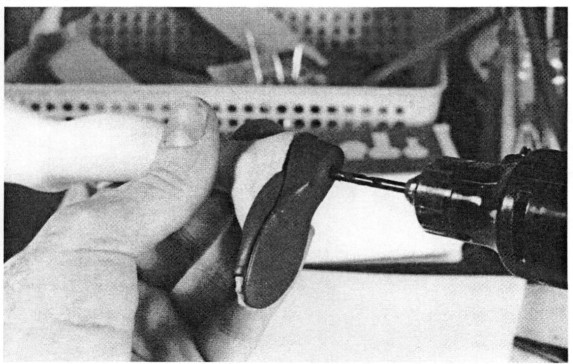

figure 35: Copper tubes are inserted and glued into these holes. Each tube will accept a steel rod which will fit into a corresponding hole drilled into a base built to hold the figure securely.

figure 36: Push the legs onto the armature wires clipping the wire so that the distance from the top of each leg matches the diagram and the figure balances on her feet.

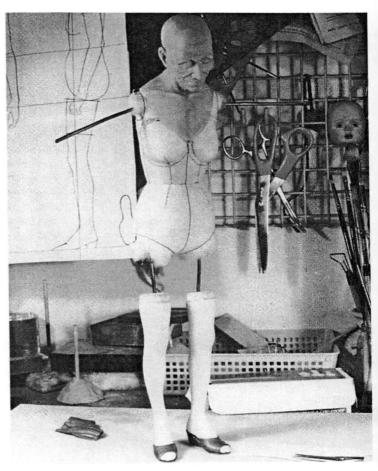

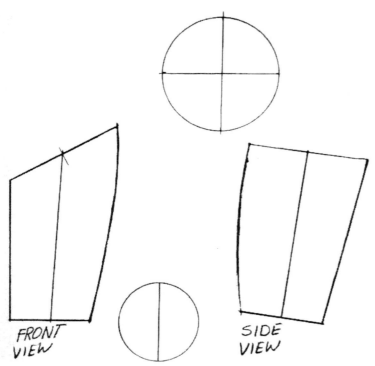

figure 37: Using the diagram, trace the front and side view of the thigh from the top of the leg to the hip. Draw a circle the size of the leg at the top and another the size of the hip.

FRONT VIEW

SIDE VIEW

figure 38: Make an armature for the thigh just as the body and leg armatures were made and glue the pieces together.

figure 39: Cut two pieces of muslin about 5 1/2" X 5" and mark a straight line through the center of each. Line up the centers with and pin them to the inside edge of each thigh. Smooth the muslin on each thigh armature toward the side, pinning it to the hip and leg disks as you go. Mark between the pins.

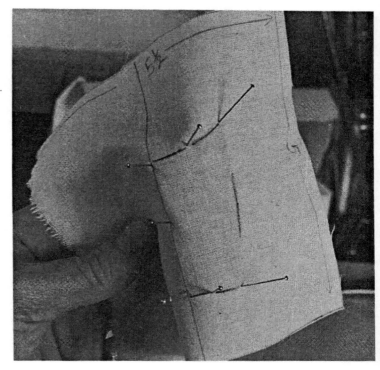

figure 40: Pad out the sections a bit with fiberfil and continue to pin and mark to the side edge. Repeat for the other side of each thigh.

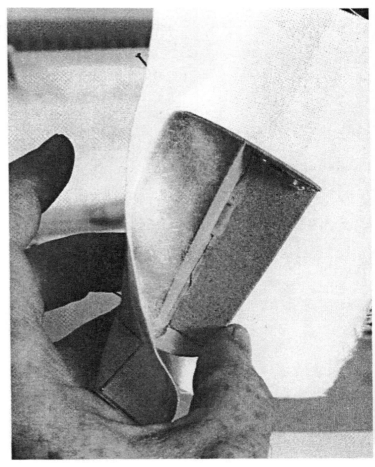

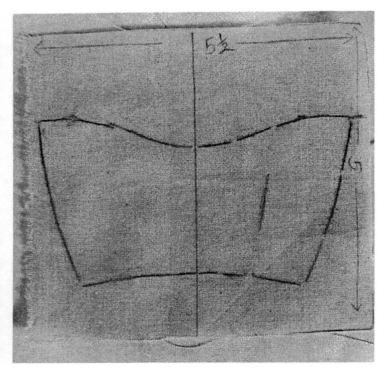

figure 41: Unpin the muslin and press. Smooth out the pencil lines. A muslin thigh is generally symmetrical on a leg in a standing position, the center being the inner thigh line.

figure 42: Cut the thigh patterns out of muslin adding 1/4" seam allowance. Stitch a guide on the seam line at the hip and the bottom of each pattern where it will join the leg. Stitch the side seam, press the seam open.

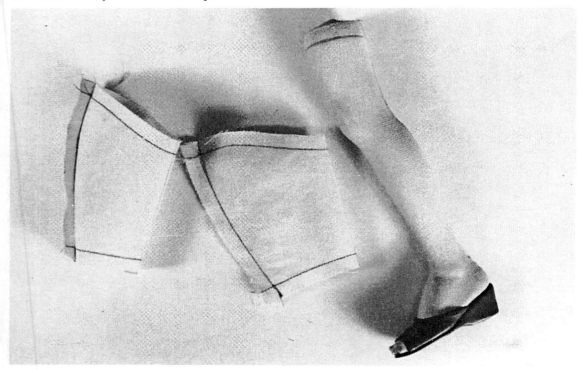

figure 43: With the right side of the muslin to the inside of a leg, pull the thigh down over the lower leg. Be sure the inner thigh is on the inside of the leg and the side seam lines up with the side of the leg. Put a good amount of glue in the groove at the top of the leg; line up the stitched guide line and force it into the groove. Place a piece of fine gauge copper wire in the groove and twist it to hold the muslin in the groove tightly.

figure 44: When the glue is dry, pull the muslin up to form the thigh.

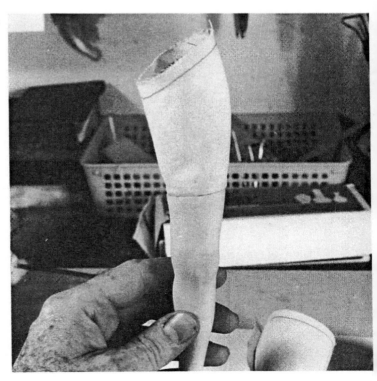

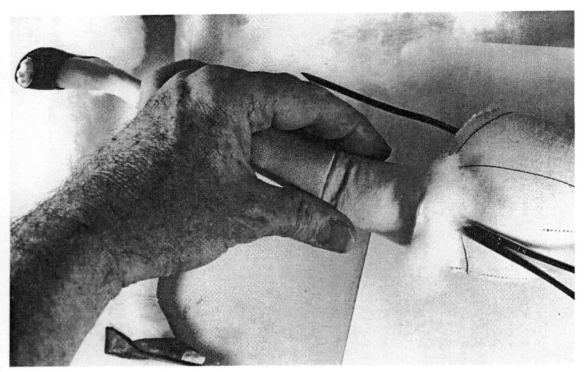

figure 45: Glue the armature wire into the leg with 5-minute epoxy and stuff the thigh firmly with fiberfil.

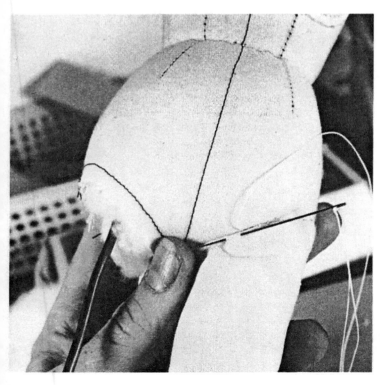

figure 46: Turn under the seam allowance of the thigh where it joins the hip and stitch it to the hip. Use a good heavy four-cord carpet thread.

figure 47: Repeat for the other leg. Stitching the thigh to the hip is a bit difficult with the first leg already in place, but it can be done.

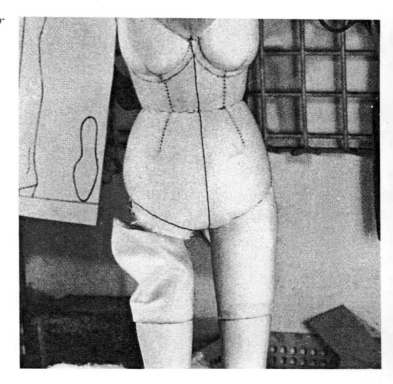

figure 48: The figure should balance nicely. If not, hold both feet to the ground and bend the torso forward or backward until it finds its balance.

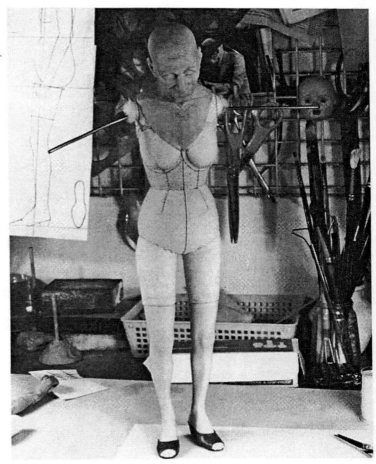

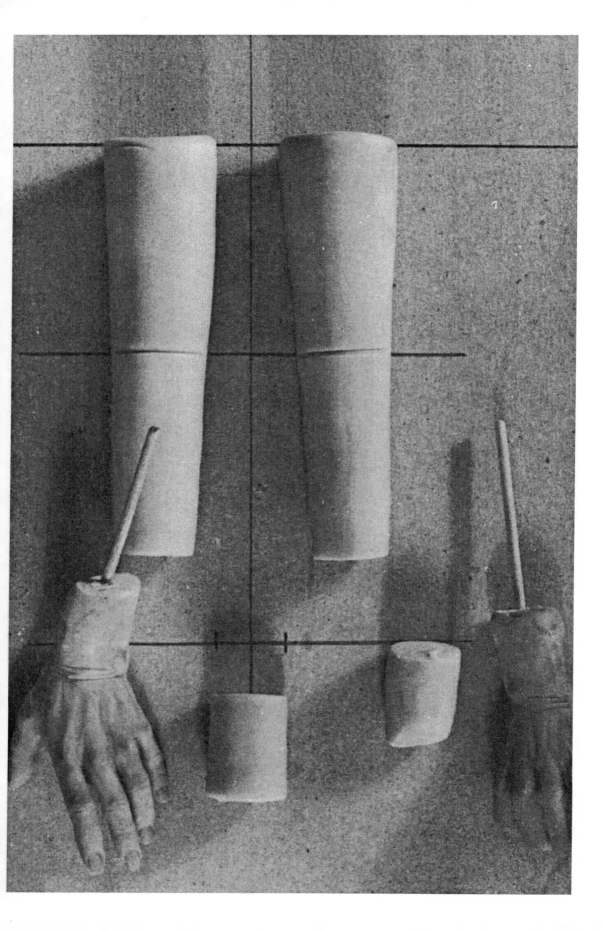

Sculpting the Hands and Arms

8

H ands are not difficult and are as fascinating as heads to do. They intimidate a lot of people, but they are as expressive as the face and in themselves are beautiful. So much character can be expressed in the hands that, in my opinion, they are as important to the success of a doll as the head.

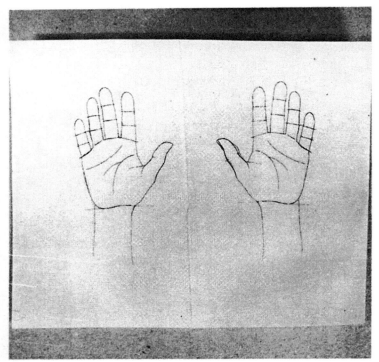

figure 1: Begin with a clear drawing of both a left and right hand. This drawing is a tracing of my hands reduced on a copy machine to the correct size. The measurement from the end of each middle or longest finger to the wrist is the same as the measurement from the chin to the hairline. I tend to make large hands, so, as always, this measurement is merely a guide—hands can be larger or smaller depending on your character.

figure 2: Using Sculpey, roll out ten coils the size of the fingers in the drawing. The little finger coils will be just slightly smaller than the other three fingers on each hand, and the thumbs slightly larger.

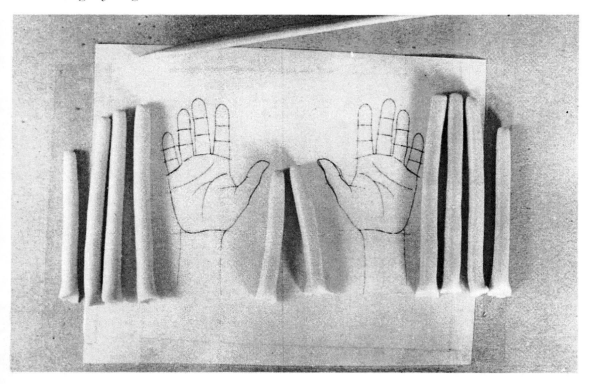

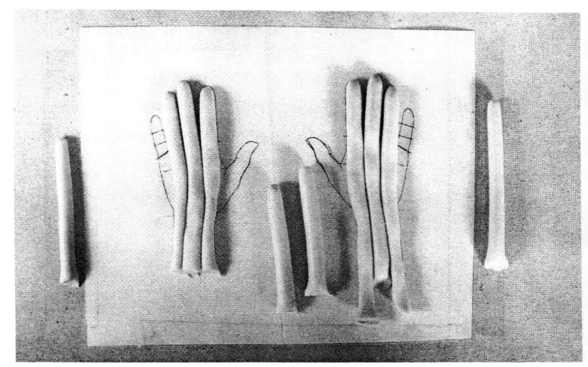

figure 3: Place coils for the three fingers other than the little finger and thumb on the drawing of each hand, matching them to the drawing exactly. The index and third fingers on each hand are the same length. The middle finger is longer than the other two. Squeeze the coils for each hand together where the palms of the hands begin.

figure 4: Mark where the fingers join the palms. Note the angle. This is very important. Blend the coils together below the marks on each hand and well past the wrists. Smooth the blending marks.

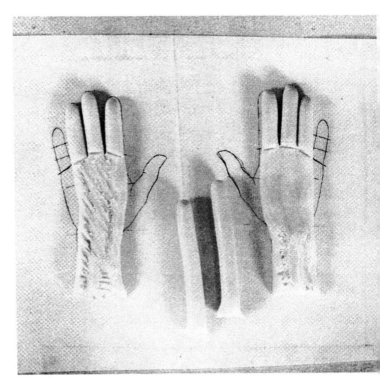

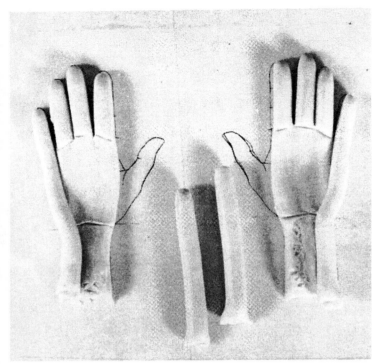

figure 5: Take the little finger coils and lay them on the drawing, about halfway down each palm. Lift the lower ends of the coils and place them on top of their respective palms and wrists.

figure 6: Shape the thumbs and place them on the drawing, matching the length of each exactly. Place the bases of the thumbs on top of the palms and wrists.

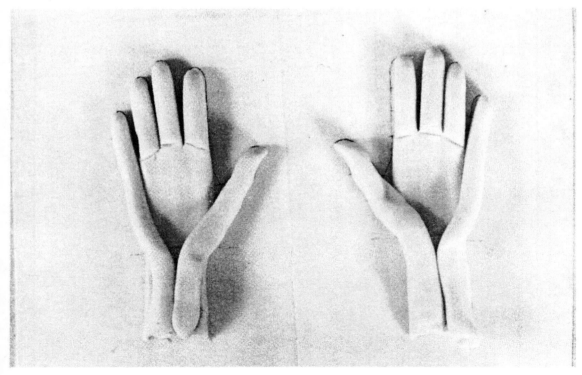

figure 7: Smooth and blend the thumbs into the palms and wrists. Mark the angle where the little finger joins each hand. Then mark where each hand joins each wrist.

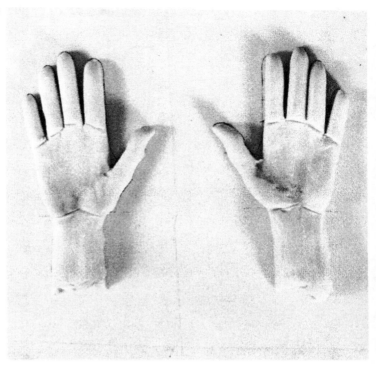

figure 8: Roll Sculpey into little flat balls and pad out the top of each palm and the base of each thumb.

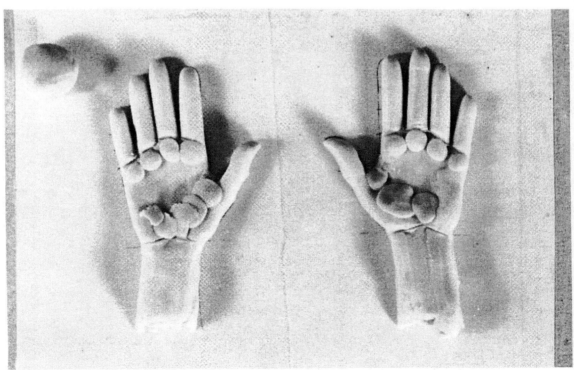

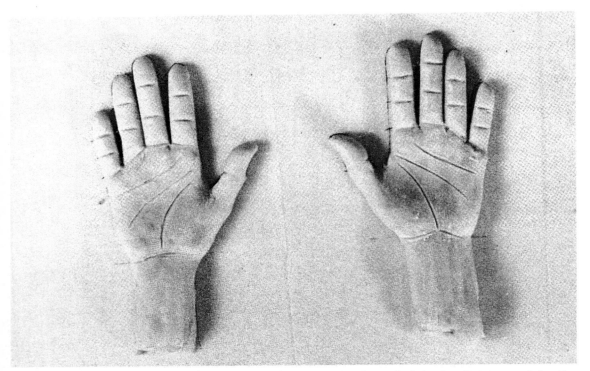

figure 9: Smooth and blend the pads into the palms. Indent slightly the divisions of the fingers, following the drawing. Indent the lines in each palm. Those lines (the ones fortune tellers read) are actually where the hands bend when they move. It is important that they be placed correctly.

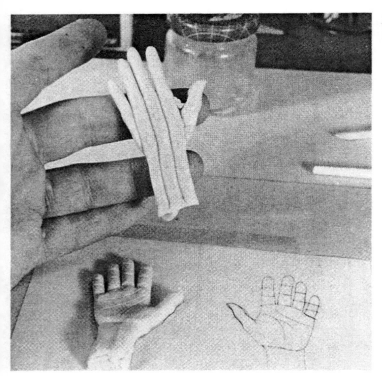

figure 10: Carefully remove the hands from the drawing and turn them over.

figure 11: Smooth the coils together on the back of the hands and roughly form the bases of the wrists.

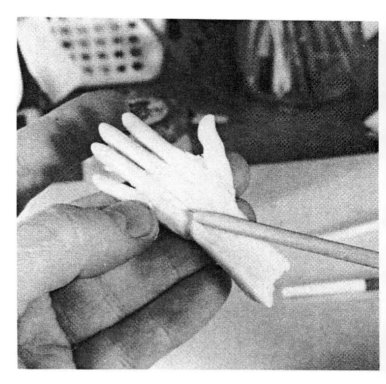

figure 12: Use the tool and flatten the end of each finger where the nail will be and mark the joints on each finger.

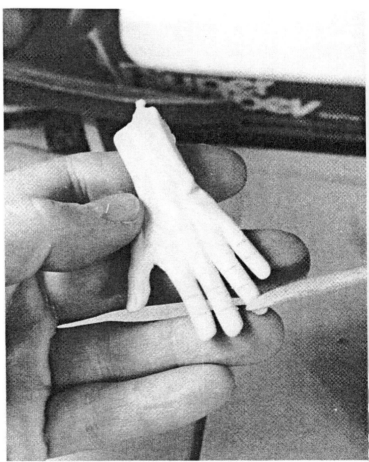

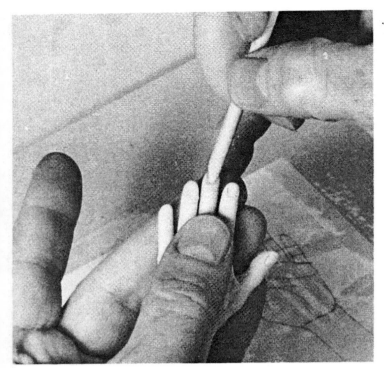

figure 13: Press into the top of each finger the shape of the nail. The base of a nail is half the distance from the end to the first joint of a finger.

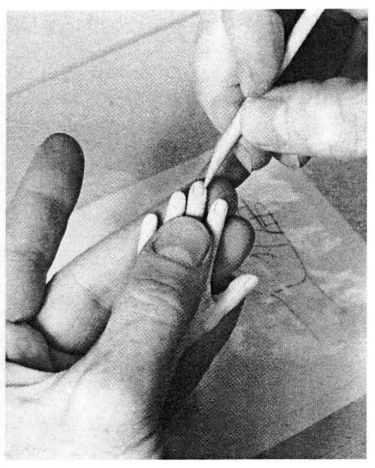

figure 14: Use the knife edge of the tool and sharply indent the sides of each nail. The nails are flat on top but indent quite sharply at the sides, the deepest part of the indentation at the end of the finger. When the nails are defined, taper the ends of each finger a little.

figure 15: The thumbs at this point are not at the correct angle to the hands. Turn them very gently so that the tops of the thumbnails are at about a 45 degree angle to each hand.

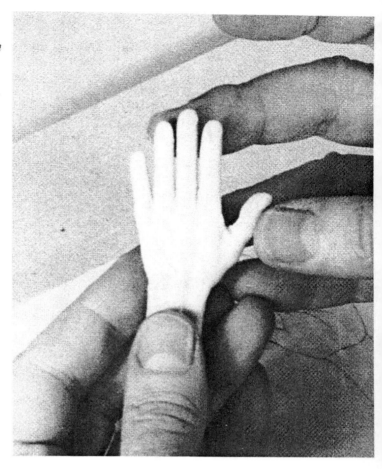

figure 16: Fingers are not round, nor are they smoothly tapered. They are actually a softly rounded square shape, wider at each joint and slightly narrower at the ends than where they join the hand. The ends are rounded. Use the tool to shape each finger slightly narrower above and below each joint.

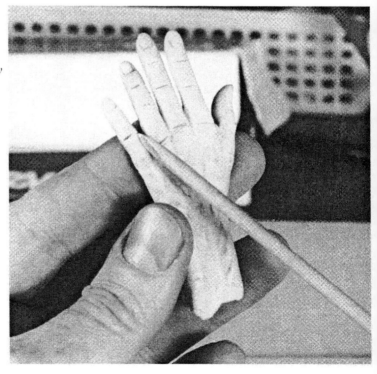

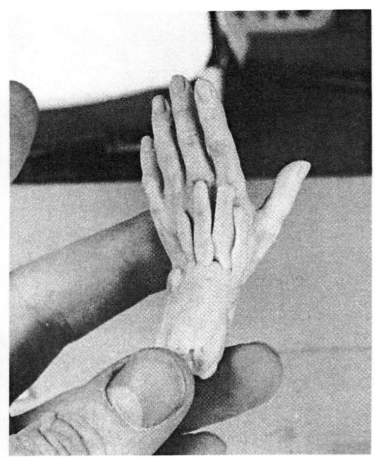

figure 17: Pose the hands the way you want them. Sculpey tends to be a little rubbery, so it must be coaxed gently. Note that fingers bend forward at the joint and that the first joint on each finger is halfway between the end of the finger and the knuckles. Cure the hands at this point so that additional detail can be added without flattening the work already done. Knuckles and leaders are then added to the top of each hand. Also note that the knuckles at the base of the fingers are not directly over the point where the palm and fingers meet, but rather they are over the first major line on the palm of each hand. Roll coils of Sculpey and add the leaders and knuckles. Hands are not flat; they are quite thick in the center where they join the wrist and taper to the knuckles.

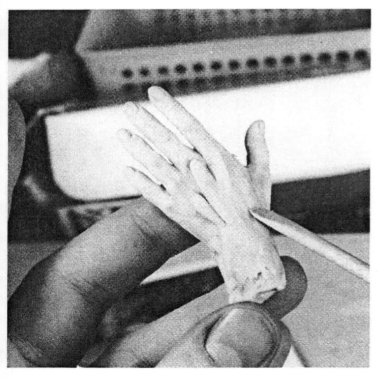

figure 18: Blend the coils into the back of each hand. Join the hands to the wrists. At this point begin to add detail and shape to the knuckles. Use your own hands as models or take pictures of hands in the poses you want.

figure 19: When the hands are finished, insert a round wooden toothpick into each wrist.

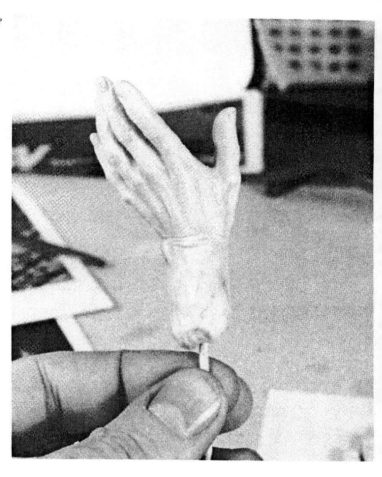

figure 20: Each toothpick should be a little less than the length of the forearms.

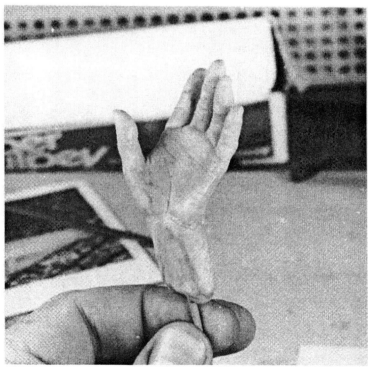

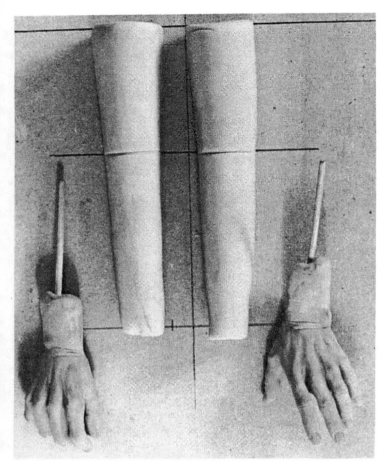

figure 21: Measure the diagram for the length of the arm from wrist to about halfway up the bicep. Mark where the elbow will be. Roll Sculpey coils the diameter of the arms. They should taper to the wrist measurement. Mark the location of each elbow.

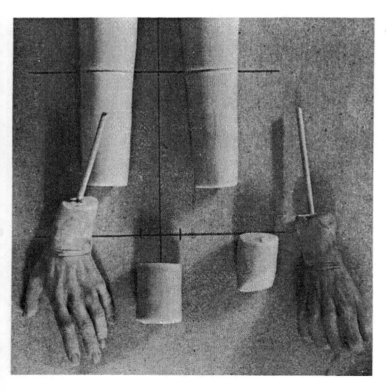

figure 22: You have already sculpted some of each forearm, so measure each and cut off that amount from the rolled coils.

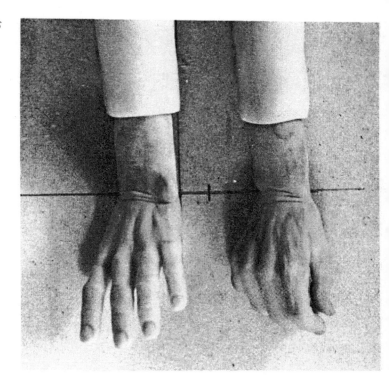

figure 23: Push the toothpicks into the arm coils and blend the coils into the wrists.

figure 24: Cut a wide notch at the inside of each elbow with an X-acto knife. The notches, at their deepest, are a little less than half the thickness of the arms at that point.

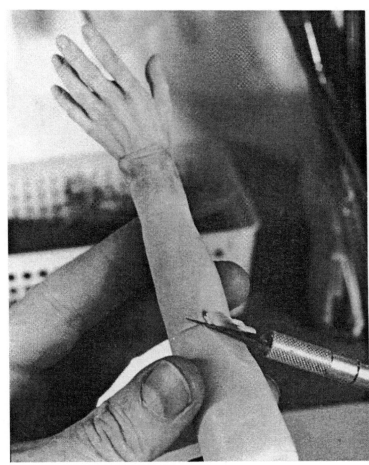

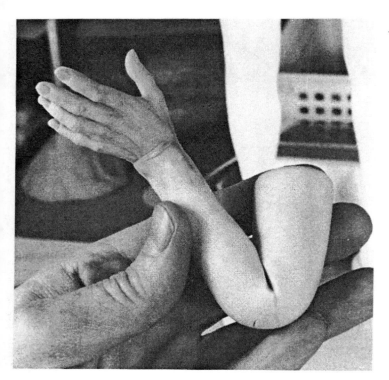

figure 25: Bend the arms at the elbows. Notice that the arms round at the elbows.

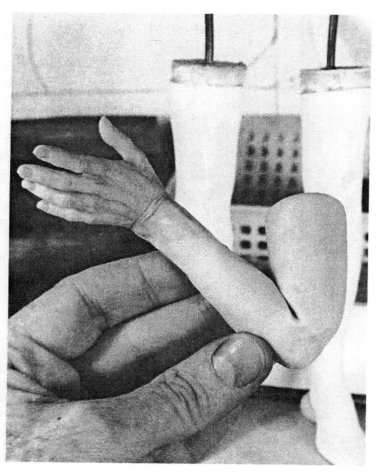

figure 26: With your forefinger and thumb, push the rounded parts into the sharp shape of elbows.

figure 27: Sculpt in the detail of the elbows if they are to show. There are sags of flesh and wrinkles around an elbow that should be put in if the figure is to wear short sleeves and the elbows are to be exposed.

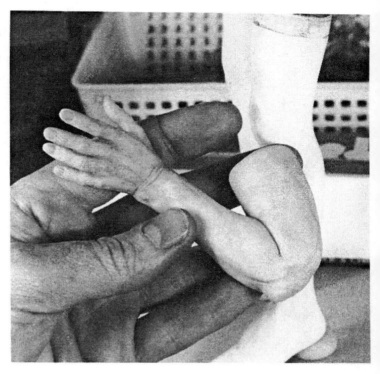

figure 28: Check the arms against the figure to make certain the poses are what you want. Indent grooves 1/4" from the top of each arm to accept the muslin upper arm. Cure the hands and arms in the oven.

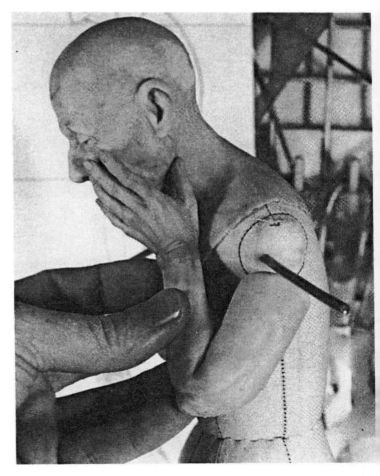

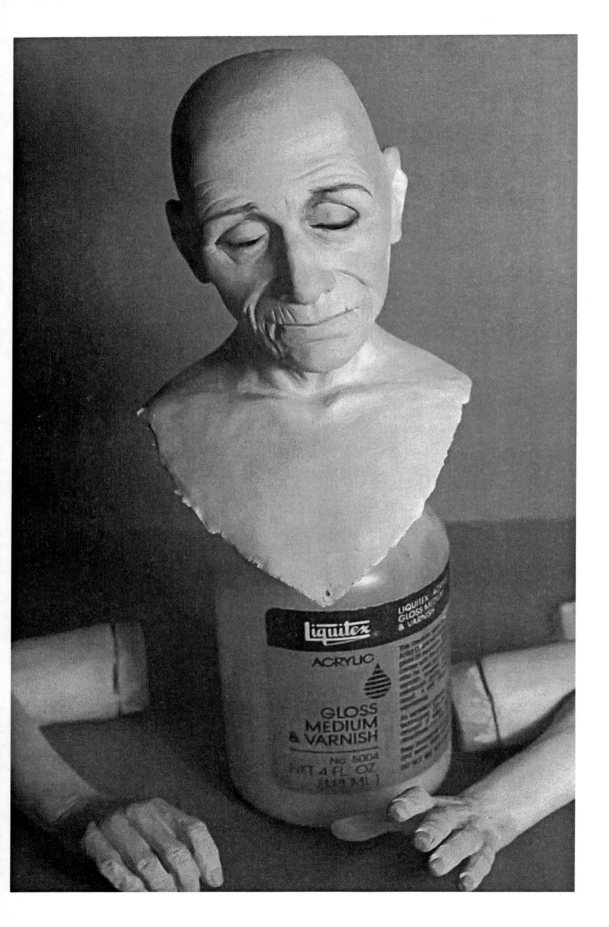

Painting the Head and Hands

9

Sculpey, if it can be kept clean throughout the sculpting process, has a terrific translucent glow when cured. I cannot keep it clean. My finished Sculpey pieces invariably look like veined marble and must be painted. I use artists' acrylics because they are durable and dry quickly. I use few colors, and a tube of paint will last a very long time. The colors I use are RED OXIDE, YELLOW OCHRE, NAPHTHOL RED LIGHT, BURNT UMBER, COBALT BLUE, and sometimes BLACK. I don't use white from the tube; I use gesso thinned with water to the consistency of cream—thin enough to brush on without running but not so thick as to leave severe brush marks.

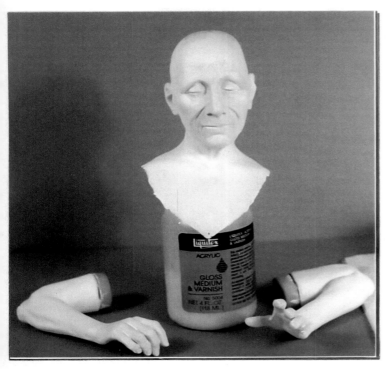

figure 1: Using a camel hair watercolor brush, give the head and hands about three coats of the thinned gesso, allowing each coat to dry before applying the rest. The gesso should be opaque, so if another coat is needed, do it.

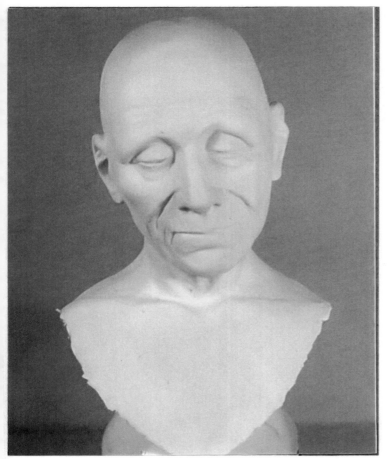

figure 2: To the thinned gesso add a small amount of RED OXIDE. Use just a drop (it is a strong color), and mix a basic flesh color. Add a touch of YELLOW OCHRE to keep the color from being too pink and a touch of COBALT BLUE to cool it slightly. Mixing the basic flesh color is strictly personal. When the color (tested on a piece of white paper and allowed to dry) satisfies your eye, paint the head. It will take three to four coats to become opaque. Don't allow the paint to fill in your detail; brush it out of the crevices and wrinkles. Blow out any bubbles that form and smooth away any brush marks.

figure 3: Thin a small amount of RED OXIDE with water to the consistency of watercolor paint and lightly brush it on the nose, the chin and ear lobes. Blend and tint these areas since flesh is not a uniform color. Use a COBALT BLUE tint with a dash of RED OXIDE and tint the eyelids very subtly. If the color dries too light, go over it again. Each time you go over a color, the deeper the tint becomes.

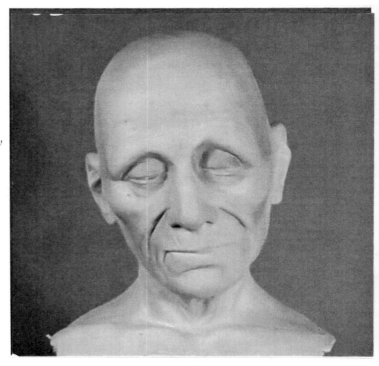

figure 4: Thin NAPHTHOL RED with water and blush the cheeks and lips. Do as many coats as necessary to get the amount of color you want. I will usually re-tint the chin and ear lobes since NAPHTHOL RED is a very pink color and looks nice over the RED OXIDE tint.

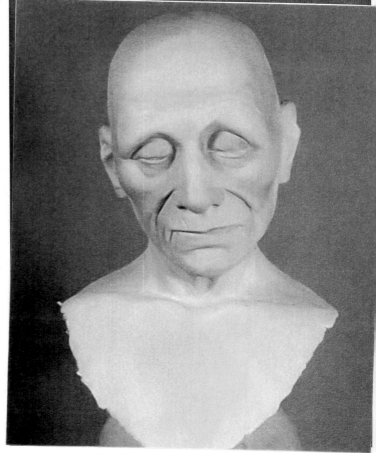

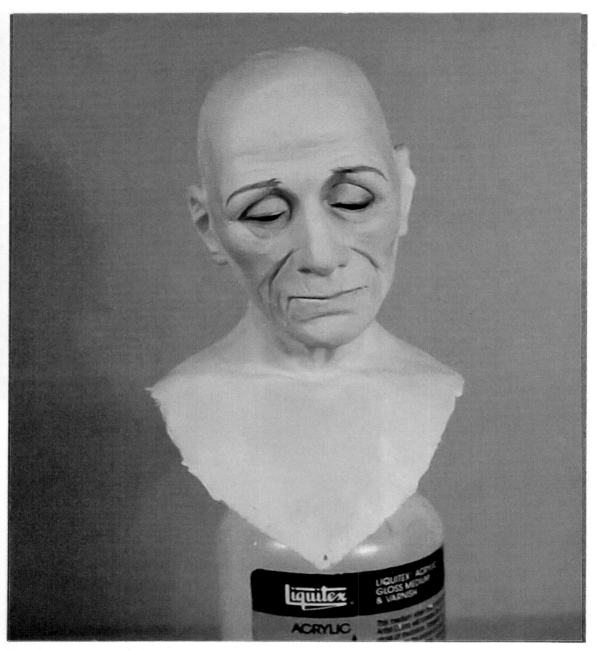

figure 5: Mix BURNT UMBER and COBALT BLUE together until you have a very deep blue-brown, almost black. I prefer this color to black; it is slightly softer and more natural look-ing. Thin it with water and begin to tint the eyebrows. Try to paint the eyebrows with many little strokes rather than an artificial single line. Deepen the crease between each eyelid and eyebrow with a couple of coats of the blue-black tint. Line the eyes. It may take up to five coats of the tint to give you the depth of color necessary, but the paint dries very quickly, and many layers of tint give a beautiful, subtle look, superior to a one stroke paint job.

figure 6: Age spots are BURNT UMBER thinned with water and put on in random splotches and sizes.

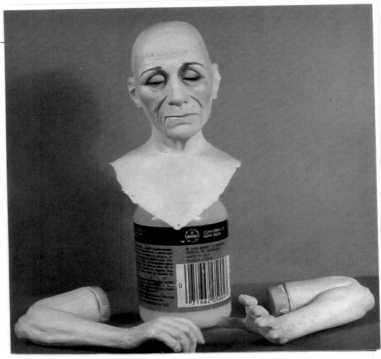

figure 7: I can quite happily glaze and tint for hours. If the blue of the eyelids bothers you, tint over it with RED OXIDE and watch it turn a gorgeous, subtle purple. If you want to emphasize the cheekbone, tint the hollows beneath with a light glaze of COBALT BLUE. Deepen the temple area with the same blue tint. At some point the head will be finished... it will tell you when.

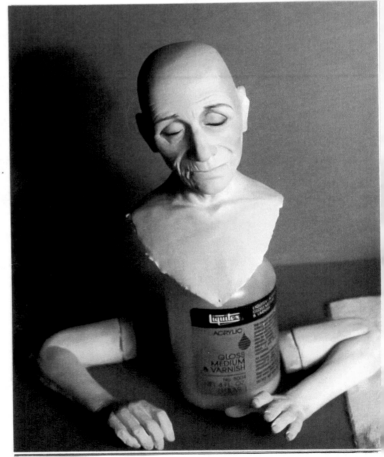

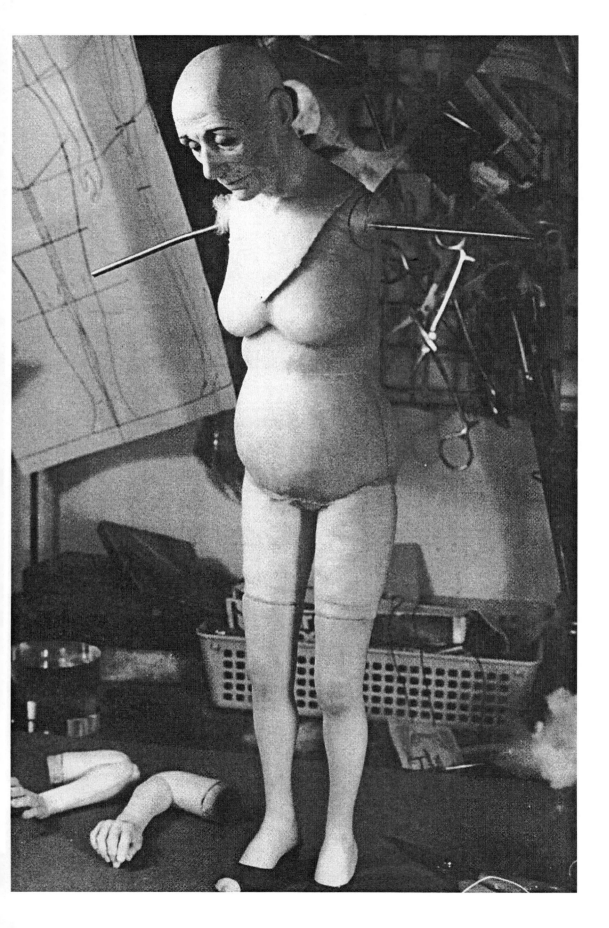

Character
Padding

10

T he stuffed muslin body of this doll is well-proportioned and the posture of the figure as I want it, but no matter how cleverly seamed and darted, a stuffed body cannot give you the rolls of flesh or the sagging breasts and buttocks of age. Padding is necessary to give the body the same character that has been sculpted into the face and hands.

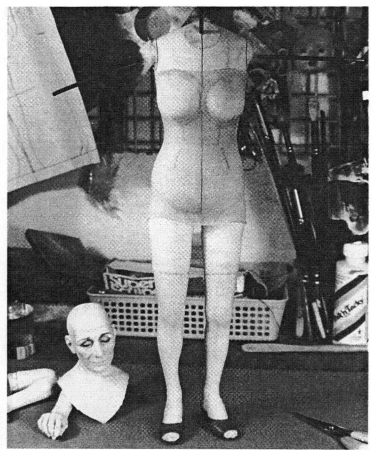

figure 1: Cut a section from a nylon hose that will reach from above the breasts to below the crotch. If the hose doesn't fit snugly enough around the body, sew a seam up the back taking in the excess for a better fit. A tube cut from a cotton t-shirt will also work but tends to be bulky and doesn't stretch as much as nylon. Slide the nylon tube over the figure and pin along the seam where the leg joins the hip.

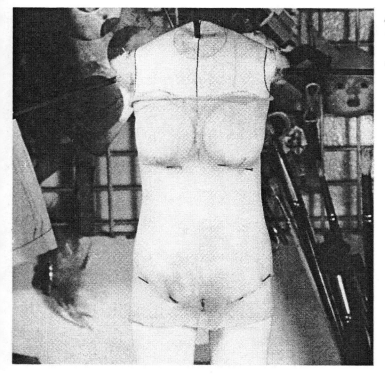

figure 2: Pad the tummy with small pieces of Fiberfil until it is the shape and size you like; pin under each breast.

figure 3: Continue to pin the tube around the lower body.

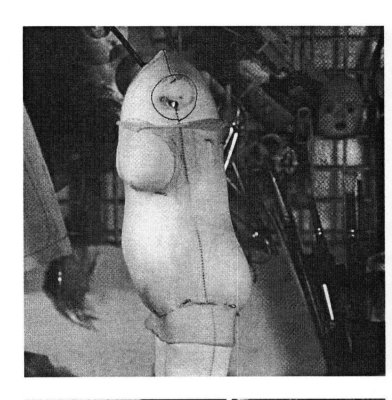

figure 4: Place a few pins along the center back line and pad out the buttocks. Hold the tube in place with a pin or two at the top.

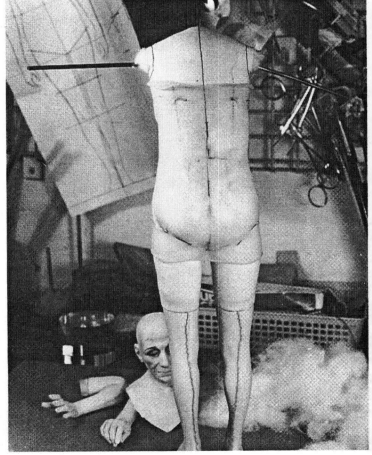

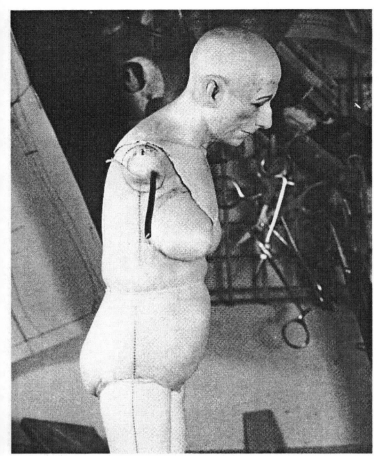

figure 5: When the tummy and buttocks are padded to the desired size and shape, stitch the tube to the muslin body along the leg seam and trim the excess nylon away. Run a line of stitches around the waist to hold the nylon to the muslin and pad above it for a little midriff bulge.

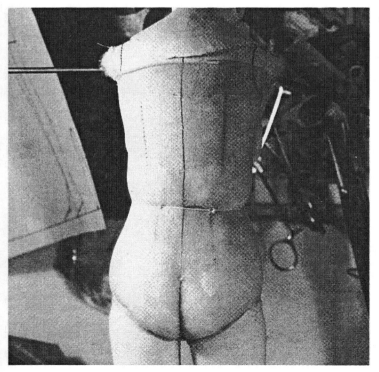

figure 6: Stitch the tube to the body beneath each breast and pad. Stitch the nylon to the hips along the center back to separate the buttocks.

figure 7: When the padding is complete, loosely tack the tube to the muslin body across the top. Smear the underside of the shoulder plate and the neck armature wire with Elmer's or 5-minute epoxy and glue the head and shoulder plate to the completed body. Secure with a pin or two and let dry.

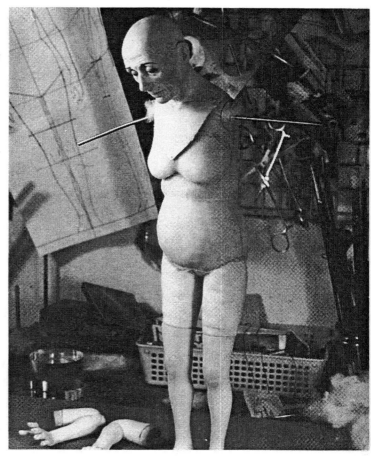

The Costume

11

S ewing a dress for a doll is very much like sewing a full scale dress. There are obviously some differences, however, due to the smaller size. The seam allowance is smaller, seldom being more than 1/4", and hems generally are 1/2". The costume is not meant to be taken off the figure; it is actually built onto it with glue or stitching, so there is no need for zippers or snap closures, and any buttons are non-functional. Only flat, un-bulky fabrics will work in scale. Facings are sometimes cut of cotton organdy to avoid bulk; however, the edges of collars will lie flatter if they are turned under and either glued or stitched rather than faced. Beautifully draped costumes are difficult to achieve even on a 24" doll since the fabric doesn't have the weight to fall nicely, but folds can be (and I do it all the time) pinned in place and steamed to give the illusion of a heavy fabric. Sleeves must be set in by hand; the armhole is so small that to get the ease into the cap evenly would be very difficult, if not impossible. However, the success of any costume begins with an accurate pattern, and the best way to achieve an accurate pattern—full scale or not—is to drape it in muslin just as the pattern for the body itself was done.

Also included in this chapter on costuming are steps for making a slip and underpants. I do not know why people insist that dolls wear underwear. Slips I understand. They can show beneath a skirt, but why panties? It seems to me anyone who lifts a doll's skirt to see if indeed she is wearing underpants has a few problems, but everybody (including myself, I admit) does it.

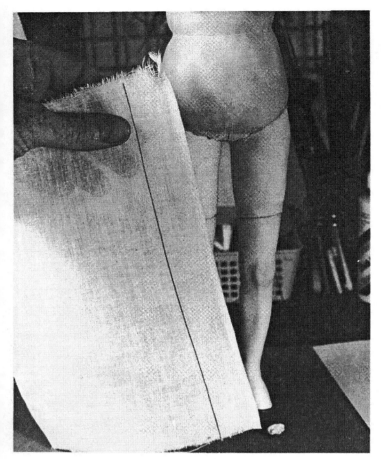

figure 1: The first pattern needed is the slip pattern. The pattern for the underpants will be drafted from the slip pattern. To begin cut a piece of muslin about 2" longer than the measurement from the waist to about where the skirt will be hemmed. Mark a line on the length 1/2" from the raw edge on the straight grain of the muslin.

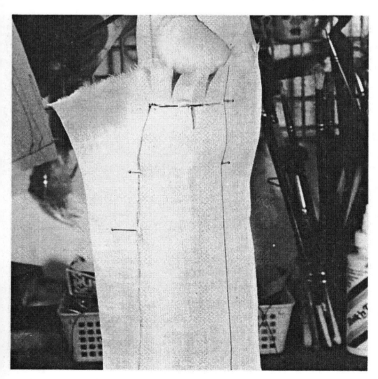

figure 2: Line up the mark on the muslin on the center front line of the body and pin it at the waist allowing about an inch of excess muslin above the waist. Put another pin through the muslin at the center line about midway down the hip section. Smooth the muslin over toward the side seam, keeping the grain of the muslin at right angles to the center front line. Pin the muslin at the side and smooth it up the side to the waist, pinning as you go. Form a dart at the waistline. Mark the waist, the dart, and the side seam with a soft pencil.

figure 3: Follow this exact procedure for the back. Pin and mark.

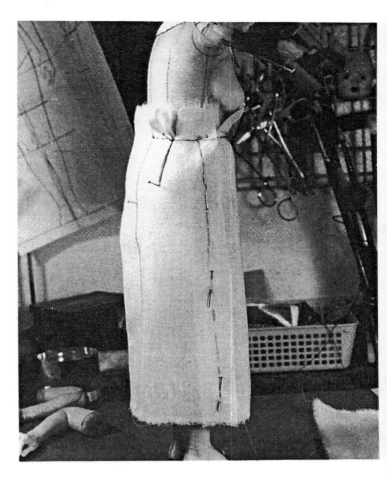

figure 4: Take the hem exactly as if this were a full scale dress.

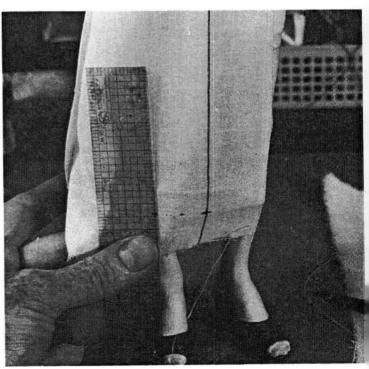

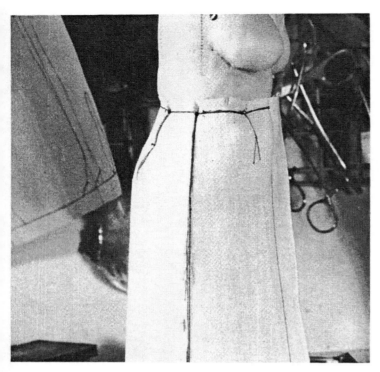

figure 5: Take the muslin off the figure, press and trim off the excess at waist and side leaving about 1/4" to 3/8" seam allowance. Either pin or baste the darts closed and the side seam together, and put it back on the figure, pinning it at center front and center back. The dress will be draped over the slip to ensure that it will fit smoothly.

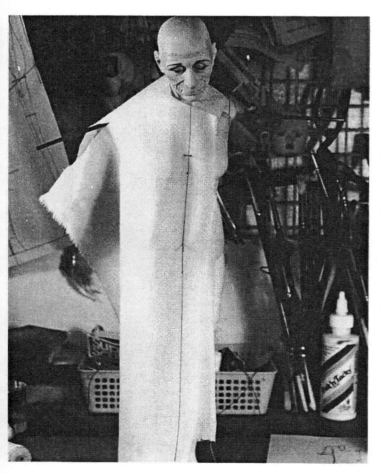

figure 6: The dress I want to put on this particular doll is one that once was called a house dress. It has no waist seam but two long side darts for just a little fit, and it buttons up the front. To begin making the pattern cut a piece of muslin long enough to reach from the neck to the ankles, adding an inch or so for the slope of the shoulder. Mark the straight grain about an inch from the raw edge. Cut a roughly shaped neck opening at the top center; slash the muslin from the side to allow it to fit over the armature wire where the armhole will eventually be. Pin it to the figure in a few places on the center front line.

figure 7: Put a pin in the center of the breast; everything will pivot from this point. Smooth and pin the muslin over the shoulder and down the side seam to where the dart will be. Smooth the muslin over the front to the side seam and down to the waist. The dart will form automatically. Pin it closed from the side seam to the bust point. Curve it slightly into the waistline to fit the front—just a little, however, so the dress will look like it is fitted—not just a loose hanging sack.

figure 8: Beginning the dart at the shoulder blade, use the same procedure for the back of the dress. Mark the shoulder seam, the armhole, and the side seam. Pin a cat's eye dart at the waist for a little fit.

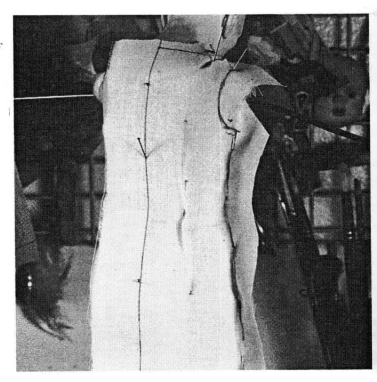

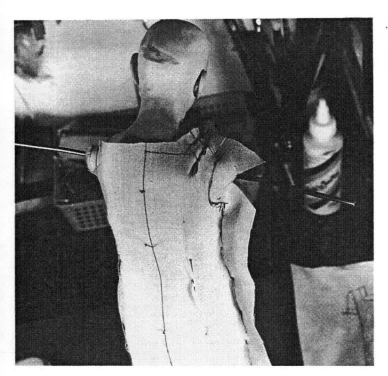

figure 9: Draw in the neck-line—in this case a square neck with an eyelet collar in the front.

figure 10: Take all the muslin pieces off the figure, press them and true up the lines with a ruler. Trace off the pattern onto heavy paper.

figure 11: To make panties trace around the top half of the slip pattern. Measure the depth of the crotch on the figure and mark it on the center front of the slip pattern. Draw a line at a right angle to center front at the depth of the crotch mark. Mark it at about one inch and drop a line parallel to the center front. At the widest part of the hip, draw a curved line from center front to inseam. Curve the inseam a bit to fit the leg more closely; otherwise the pants will fit like culottes. Figure the length and mark it on the pattern. Use the same procedure for the back.

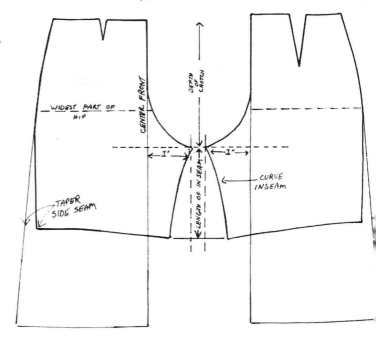

figure 12: Cut the underpants of whatever fabric you have chosen (tricot from an old slip and cotton batiste are great) and stitch them up, trimming with lace if you wish. Leave the center back seam open enough to allow the pants to slip onto the figure easily. Press all seams open and put the pants on the doll. If the panty leg is too full, pin it out of the side seam and the inseam. Stitch the panties onto the figure at the waist with long running stitches.

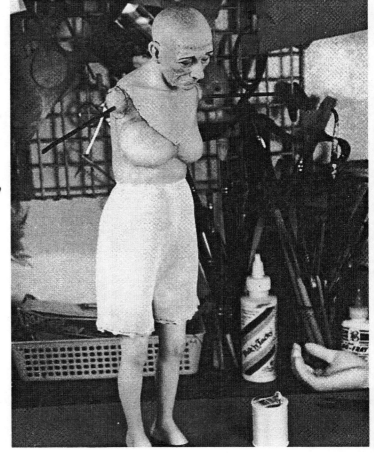

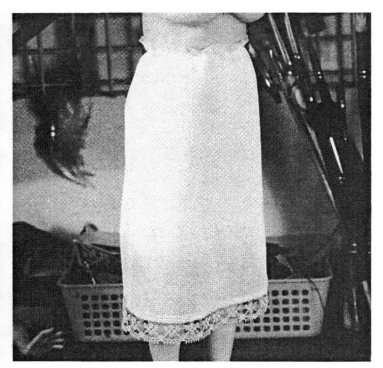

figure 13: Cut the slip out of the same fabric as the panties and stitch up, adding lace trim as you go; slip it onto the figure. Stitch to the figure at the waist.

figure 14: The dress is cut out and stitched, the collar is applied but not faced, the pockets are placed but not stitched. If the fit needs correcting, now is the time to do it. Once the fit is right, the pockets are stitched on, the neckline is faced, and the hem is turned up.

figure 15: Except for the buttons and sleeves the dress is finished; it is at this point that I attach the arms.

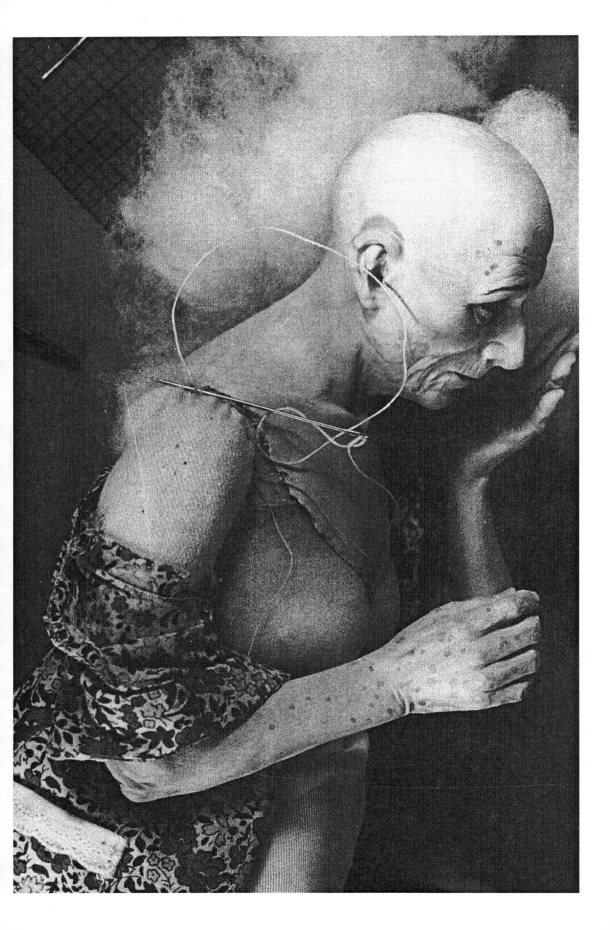

Attaching the Arms

12

Because of the way contemporary clothes fit the human figure and because this doll is not fully articulated, it is impossible to slip a dress with set-in sleeves onto the doll after the arms are attached to the body. Therefore, once the body of the dress is already on the doll, I make the upper arms, attach them to the lower arms, and attach the arms, whole, to the body. The upper arm, made of muslin, could be drafted from measurement; but it would be guesswork, so it is necessary to make one more cardboard armature upon which to shape the upper arm pattern. It seems like the hard way to do this, but in the long run it is faster and more accurate than drafting.

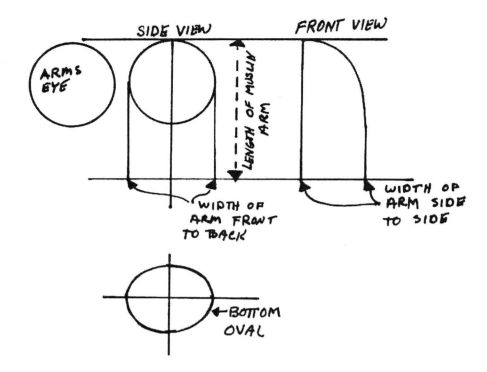

SIDE VIEW

FRONT VIEW

ARMS
EYE

LENGTH OF MUSLIN ARM

WIDTH OF
ARM FRONT
TO BACK

WIDTH OF
ARM SIDE
TO SIDE

BOTTOM
OVAL

figure 1: To make an armature for the upper arm pattern, draw a circle the size of the armhole on the torso. Drop a straight line through the center of the circle the same length as the distance from the top of the shoulder to where the muslin upper arm will join the sculpted lower arm. Draw another line at right angles to the first at that point. Mark the width of the sculpted arm equal distance from the center line and connect with the circle. This is the side view of the arm. Draw another line the length of the muslin arm and another at right angles where the join will be. Measure the width of the sculpted arm and mark it on that line. Connect that mark to the top of the shoulder curving it to give the shoulder the correct shape. This is the front view. Since the width of the arm from side to side is less than the width from front to back, the bottom piece of the armature will be an oval rather than a circle. Mark two lines at right angles to each other and mark the side to side measurements on one and the front to back measurements on the other equal distances from the center where the lines intersect. Draw a smooth oval.

figure 2: Transfer the armature pieces to cardboard and cut them out. Glue the pieces together as was done with the body armature.

figure 3: Cut a rectangle of muslin a bit larger in length and width than the armature and mark a line down the center on the straight grain. Pin the muslin on the armature with the center line on the curved edge of the FRONT VIEW. Pin around the bottom oval and pin the top circle to the opposite edge of the front view. Mark as you go. Since the pattern will be symmetrical, it isn't necessary to pin the muslin to the back of the armature.

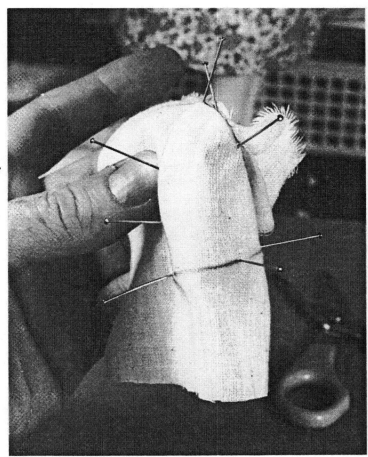

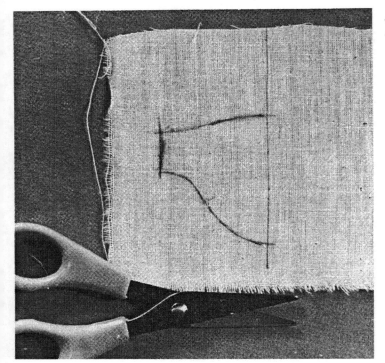

figure 4: Unpin the muslin and press. Smooth out the lines, fold the muslin in half on the center line, add 1/4" seam allowance, and there's the pattern.

figure 5: Drill a hole in the sculpted arm to accept the armature wire. Slide the arm on the wire and measure to make sure the distance from the top of the shoulder to the elbow matches the diagram. Cut the upper arms out of muslin; put a machine basting stitch around the cap to ease it onto the armhole. Press the seam open.

figure 6: Slide the muslin, wrong side out, onto the arm making sure the seam is on the inside of the arm. Glue the bottom seam allowance into the groove and secure with a piece of carpet thread or fine wire.

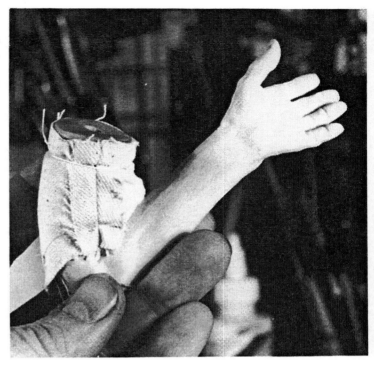

figure 7: Pull the muslin up, turning it right side out.

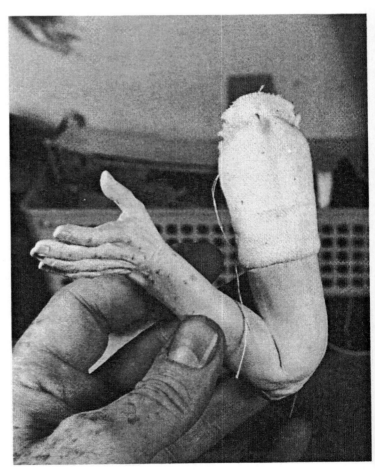

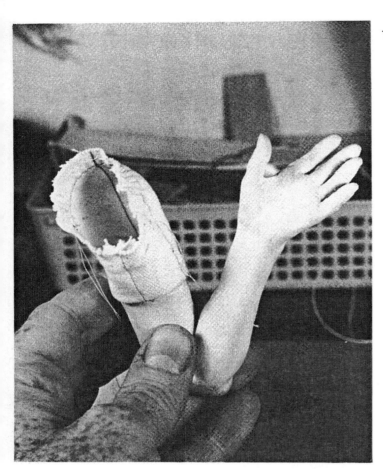

figure 8: Pull the machine basting stitch to form the ease in the cap.

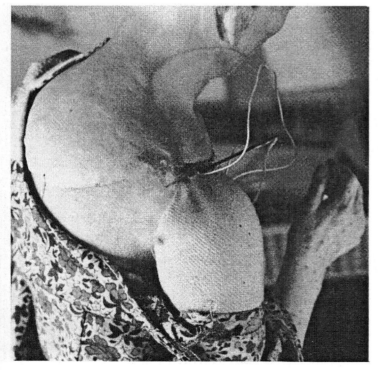

figure 9: Slide the armature wire through the muslin upper arm into the hole in the lower arm and glue. Stuff the muslin arm keeping it as smooth as possible. Pin the armhole of the dress out of the way, and with the seam allowance turned under, pin the muslin upper arm to the armhole of the body matching the center line to the shoulder seam.

figure 10: Hand stitch the muslin arm to the body, easing in the cap as you go. It may be necessary to add a bit more Fiberfil to smooth out the cap.

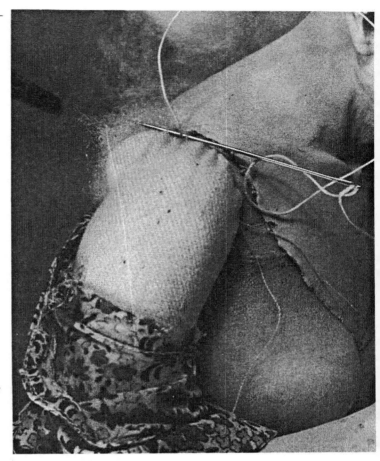

figure 11: When both the arms are attached, tack the seam allowance of each dress armhole to the muslin arm at the shoulder.

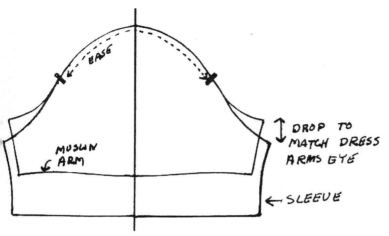

figure 12: The sleeves use the same pattern as the muslin upper arm, but in order for the sleeve to cover the connecting seam, it must be cut longer and about 3/8" wider for ease around the arm. Drop the cap of each sleeve at the seam to match the armhole on the dress.

figure 13: Cut the sleeves out of the dress fabric. Place a machine stitch around each cap from notch to notch. Hem or trim the bottom edge and stitch the seam closed.

figure 14: Turn the seam allowance under and slip the sleeve over the hand and onto the arm.

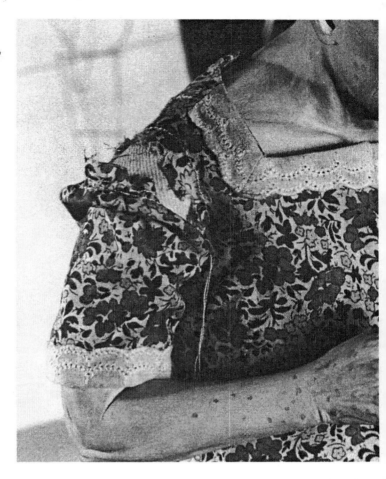

figure 15: Match the seam of the sleeve to the dress side seam and the top of the cap to the shoulder seam. Pin the sleeve in place and hand stitch to the dress. This is a hassle to do, but the arm can be bent out of the way to make it a bit easier to get to the seam. Take very tiny ladder stitches; when finished, bend the arm back into place.

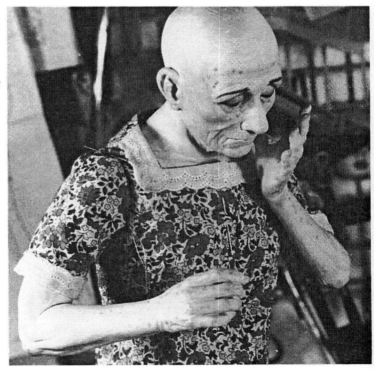

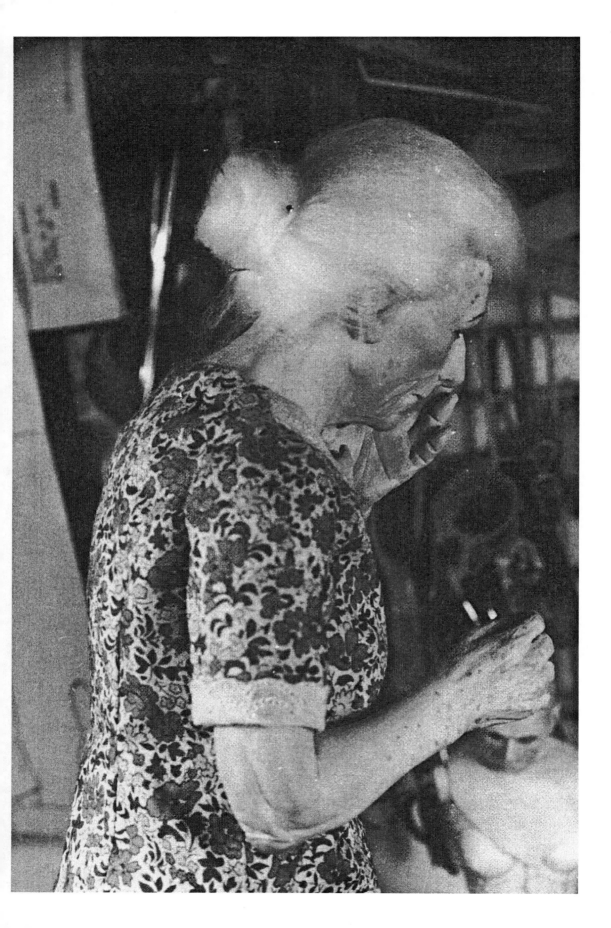

The Hair

13

Wigs are difficult, I don't care what anybody says! The stuff one must use is maddening to handle, but the end results are worth the agony. Never, repeat, never use human hair nor, except on rare occasions, manmade fiber made for human wigs. In all but the largest dolls the hairs from a human wig are simply out of scale. I use mohair or crepe hair, both of which are fine enough to be in scale to the doll and can be curled or arranged into a nice approximation of a contemporary hair style. The style for this doll is simple—the hair is pulled back into a neat little bun at the back of the head. This style is the simplest for me to do and fits the character of the doll. I don't make wigs with wig caps. I glue the hair directly to the head. Once styled, it cannot be changed. Wig caps are time consuming and usually look like wigs rather than a head of hair.

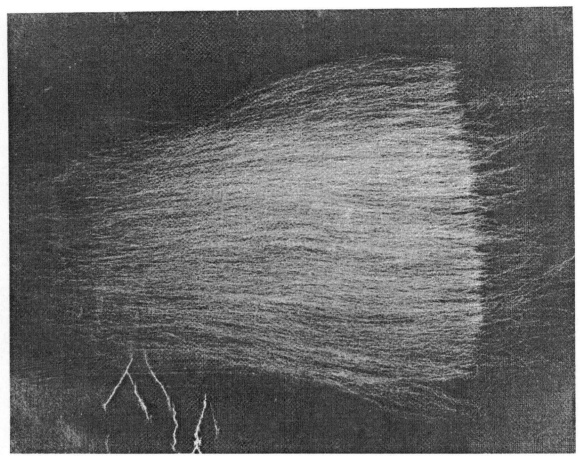

figure 1: Using a length of the material you have chosen from which to make the wig, cut 4" lengths, or separate by holding the material with both hands about 4" apart and giving a tug . Spread the lengths into 1 1/2" or 2" widths and lay these next to each other on a piece of waxed paper. Comb the hair until it is smooth. To do this you can use a fine toothed comb, a toothbrush, or even a tapestry needle. You will comb out a great deal of excess. Put it aside and don't be alarmed at the amount. Keep combing until the length of hair is spread flat and smooth, all tangles removed.

figure 2: Stitch through the hair and waxed paper using the smallest stitch on your sewing machine.

figure 3: Pull the waxed paper apart at the stitched line. Run a line of white glue through the stitches and the ends of the hair. When the glue is dry, trim the edge close to the stitches.

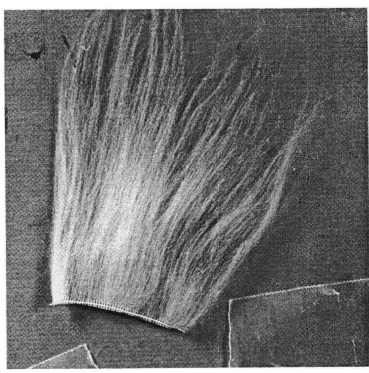

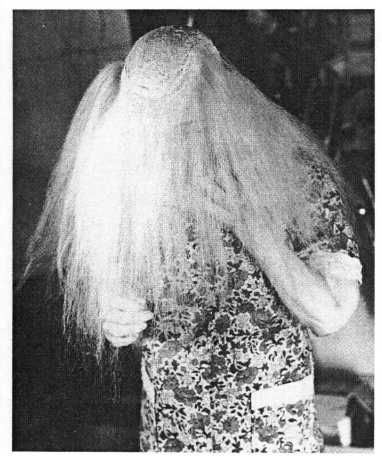

figure 4: Use a colored pencil that matches the color of your wig and mark the hairline all around the head. Paint the skull to match the color of the hair. Take the stitched hair and glue it to the head at the hairline using tacky glue. Don't begin to style the hair until the glue is really dry.

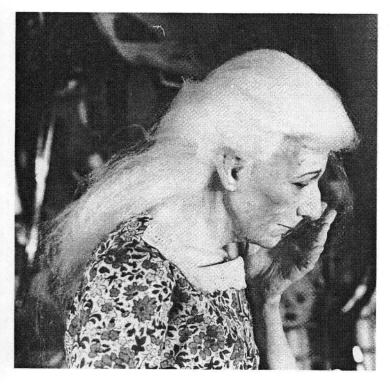

figure 5: Using a tapestry needle, begin to pull the hair away from the face toward the back of the head.

figure 6: Don't comb the hair absolutely smooth and sleek like a cap, rather, pull some strands tighter than others for a more natural look. Soften the hairline by pulling tendrils out, especially around the sides.

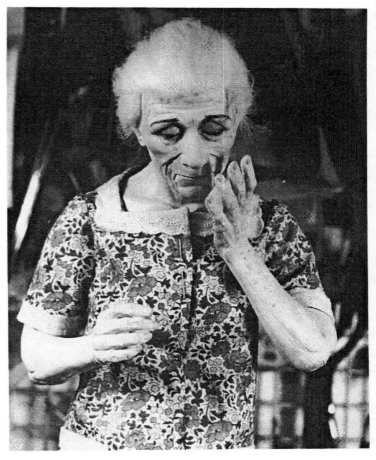

figure 7: Twist the hair into a bun in the back and secure with a few pins.

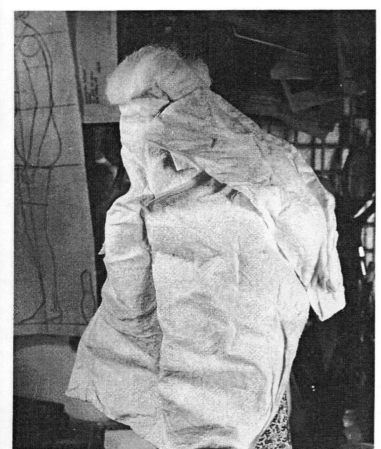

figure 8: Wrap the doll in paper towels to protect it, being very careful to mask the face, ears and neck. Use hair spray for hard to hold hair, giving the hair a light mist. Let dry and mist again. It will take about three or four mistings to really secure the hair. The spray may bead up on separate hairs but the beads usually disappear when the spray dries.

figure 9: When the hair is completely dry, remove the paper towel and the doll is complete, ready for her base.

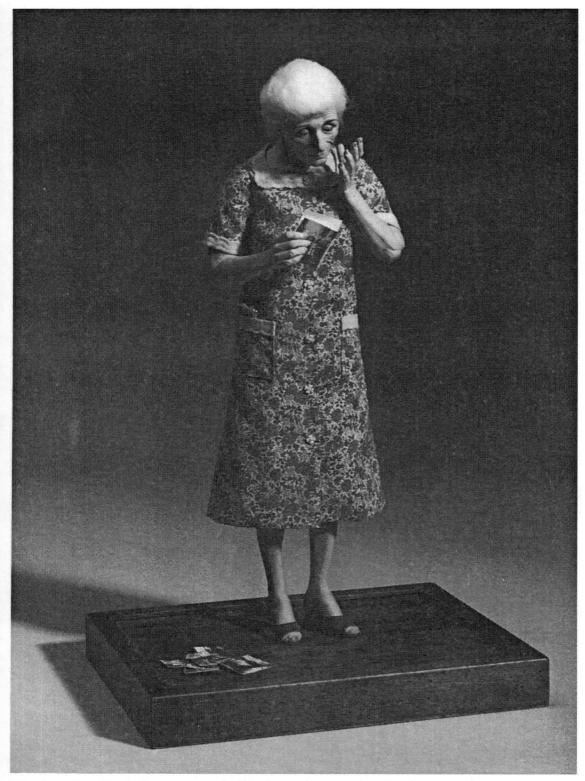

The base for this doll is a piece of 3/4" plywood covered with a bass wood veneer and framed with an inexpensive standard size frame refinished to match the veneer. Holes are drilled into the base to accept two brass rods that extend into each leg to allow the figure to stand without tipping over.